I0559089

6928 Thomas Boulevard

Memories of a Pittsburgh Boyhood

by

Elliott Maloney

Contents

DEDICATION

To my sibs
Bobbi, Maureen
Jim, Billy and Mike
You give joy to my heart!

INTRODUCTION

When I was a youngster, it was a very good time to be child. It was the 1950's after all. And it really helped if you were a white boy of the middle class, and you hit the jackpot if you were part of a happy two-parent family and lived in a good part of town. I was lucky like that. I have wondered about my generation, the Baby Boomers (I was born about nine months after the Japanese surrender in World War II), why so many of us grew up happy and have "done well" in life in many areas. I wonder, too, why so many others of us have become disillusioned, lost our religious affiliation, and live tortured lives. And why we have reared so many unmotivated, confused children.

I've always wanted to write about what it was like growing up in the pleasant Point Breeze section of the fine city of Pittsburgh. I look back in wonder at those days, at the course of my childhood, with its great serenity, its innocent yet rich relationships, the calming surety of knowing where you belonged and what you were supposed to do.

I am happy to admit that the final inspiration to write of these fond memories came to me from Annie Dillard's wonderful book, An American Childhood. When I read that excellent tome and realized that it was all about a neighborhood just a few blocks from our home in Pittsburgh, I jumped out of my chair and said aloud, "She's the Protestant girl and I'm the Catholic boy she writes of. I can tell the other side of the story she was always wondering about—and our stories are better!" When I saw that some of the people she wrote about were ones that I knew or knew of, something broke open in me that would not be contained until I put down on paper as much of our story as I could.

Well, that was back in 1990. I jotted down some episodes that had to be in it, like Mom, Dad, Church, the Sisters, Monsignor and a about ten others, but in those days I was so busy with school and scholarship,

I let the idea slide (but continue percolating) until I had a sabbatical in the Spring of 1997, at our Priory in Brazil of all places. There it was that I borrowed the house's computer and started writing some fifteen more vignettes. Luckily, I printed them all out on the 30x21 centimeter paper they use there, because I had a heck of a time finding a machine to read the diskettes I saved them on! For some reason, I started editing some of them and adding a few more in September of 2021 when I cut back on my teaching load after my seventy-fifth birthday. But now I have picked the thing up again, to review and polish up some two and a half dozen mini-chapters that I had in various stages of completion and saved in various places.

Well, this book is about our home, a great big lovely yellow brick mansion with an enormous front porch on a beautiful street in a fine neighborhood in the best of all times to have grown up in the U.S.A. No, this is not a new version of A Tale of Two Cities or a kind of twenty-first century Candide. I think that what I just wrote is actually true for the most part. That was just the reality of our experience and circumstances back then!

Of course, this book is not actually about a house that once stood at 6928 Thomas Boulevard, but that house is a symbol of all that was good in my "American Childhood." Its rooms and neighborhood haunts are what I dream about when I have to work out something important in my sleep. Everything I value in my life began in some way back there, in and around 6928 Thomas Boulevard. And even though the house is long gone from its noble site, it still exists in my imagination, in great detail as you will see. I cherish the memories and want to share as much as I can of the warmth and security of those halcyon days.

I'm not a sociologist, psychologist, or practitioner of any of the hard or soft sciences, but many years of academic study and teaching of the Bible have shown me that a lot of insight can come from the stories of religious people. And I think that if we can touch again what made us so happy in the past, we might be able to make part of it happen again today.

I have, therefore, not tried to write an autobiography, but rather to illustrate from the life of one family the way it was back then, and to indicate some of the many ways we lived out what we believed to be good and true. I will present our story without too much exaggeration or honeycoating, but honestly as I remember things, with no fabrications out of thin air, on one hand, but without all the fact-checking needed for a documentary, on the other. Just the honest description of the way I remember my childhood. The parameters of the book are easy to define: it begins with my early memory of going to kindergarten in the Fall of 1951. The end point is our move to Buffalo, New York in the summer of 1959, just after my thirteenth birthday.

I offer these stories for your pleasure. Some of the details may be fuzzy and I admit to have omitted or changed a few names, but I have basically told the truth of how we lived back then. Like any life, our life on Thomas Boulevard had joy and sorrow, but I want to share some of the good things that could make for a healthy childhood in every family the world over. As a matter of fact, without boasting or arrogance, I think that our life back then could be a model for anyone today, and more importantly, a goal for the freedom and happiness of every child in a truly just world.

Part 1 – 6928

1 – The House Itself

It was a big house, grand, one would have to say, built in 1905 as part of the "Westinghouse Park Plan," because of its proximity to the great inventor's mansion "Solitude." That estate took up the whole next block of Thomas Blvd., all the way north to the Pennsylvania Railroad main line. Since the heir turned it over to the city for use as a park only in 1919, we must suppose that our house and the other five other houses of the Plan, that took up both sides of the 6900 block of Thomas, were to create a spacious "park" setting for those residences. After all, they were advertised as dwellings for "the captains of industry" on a boulevard wide enough to be touted as reminiscent of the Champs Elysees.

The other five houses of the Plan, those of the Joyces, the Sheedys, Jamie van Trump's house, and number 6941 and the one with the big white columns nearest the Park, had all remained pretty much in the same shape as they were built when Dad bought our house, 6928, in 1948. Our house, however, had been expanded greatly by the addition of a large two-story wing on each side, turning the stately mansion into a three apartment dwelling. On the left side, a private entrance, lobby and stairwell (and much more) was added for the second floor apartment. On the right side of the house the kitchen on the first floor was considerably lengthened, and a bedroom, a hallway, and a full bathroom were added below the rather large kitchen and sunroom of the second floor apartment.

On the kitchen side of the house, too, was a small public lobby from which you could enter our kitchen; it was our back door. There, too, you opened a door to the steps down to the cellar. In the middle of that vestibule was a staircase that led up to a larger lobby on the second floor. But before you got there, off a landing toward the front of the house was a studio apartment with its own bath and kitchen. Did I mention that I had my eye on this independent abode ever since my sister Bobbi went off to the Josephite convent in Baden? What cool digs this would make for a free-spirited high school boy! Back out in the hall this cavernous well gave rear access upstairs to the kitchen of the second-floor apartment, opening as well onto the original staircase that led to a third floor. Here there was a third apartment consisting of the four rooms of the original top floor of the house without addition, but with a marvelous sundeck on top of the east wing of the house. Before you entered this apartment, on the right, toward the back of the house, was a long room that we used as our attic.

The first floor, where we lived, was large and of excellent design. In the front was the foyer (bigger than most folk's living rooms) flanked by the "good" living room and the dining room. The dining room was a stately place with its crystal chandelier and grand dimensions. Its walnut wainscoting was met at the height of a man's shoulder by a silky wallpaper of opulent clusters of purple grapes in classic urns. Two large window seats enhanced the large portals looking out to the side yard. They adorned an even more remarkable and broad mantle over a fireplace in the center. To the front, a picture window we could hardly open for its size looked out across the porch onto the boulevard. The kitchen was entered through a swinging door in the back that was absolutely lethal to childish fingers when on rare occasions it was not propped open with its wooden plane, stained, of course, to match the decor. It was here that the family ate dinner every night at "5:00 sharp—and you'd better not be late. No excuses accepted!"

On the other side of the foyer was the "good" living room, the front room, always in view through its wide opening into the foyer, but closed off from the room right behind it, a space we would today call the family room, by a set of closed pocket doors. Now there must be a reason why we called it the "good" living room, and it was probably because it had the "good" furniture and an oriental rug. All we knew was that we were never allowed in it, except at Christmas, that is, when we practically lived in it. For there stood the tree, the creche, and our enormous train set.

Both the dining room and the "good" living room opened onto the foyer with large pocket doors. They could (but didn't very often) close off the rooms by their huge sliding panels, one of walnut, to match the dining room, and the other of lightly stained oak, to match the handsome woodwork of the "good" living room. These doors, and the third set that separated the (plain old ordinary) living room, slid easily into the walls, and even as a child I always admired the effortlessness with which they could disappear from view with never a snag, never a "coming off their trolley." This house was solidly built by carpenters who must have spent half their time using their levels and tape measures!

Now the "old" living room was where we lived! It wasn't any older, of course, but I guess that that's where we had the older furniture, impervious to kids' bouncing and spilling, neither of which was allowed, of course. (RULE #2 was "No eating in the living room!" All THE RULES! ended in an exclamation point.) Here was the television set, a Westinghouse console, of course. Not only did Dad get a 25% discount on all Westinghouse appliances, but much more importantly, everyone knew that a Westinghouse was far superior to any other brand. (What a revelation it was when I found out that they were all really Zenith sets, repackaged by Westinghouse!)

In that room stood the piano, a big old mahogany upright that all us kids used to practice on. I think it was a good one, passed on from my Grandmother's house, but for the life of me I can't remember the name above the keyboard that stared me in the face for half an hour every day from second grade on. We even hauled the thing to Buffalo, but no one used it anymore—so many things changed when our childhood slipped away into adolescence.

At the rear of the foyer, outside the "old" living room, where the original staircase to the upstairs would have been, was a kind of sacred empty space punctuated only by its pink shag rug and large, black, half-round table. It is here, if we had been ancient Romans, that the household gods would have been kept, between two remnants of the ancient banister displayed against the back wall. It was here where we kids celebrated our "Mass" with white Necco wafers for hosts and a silver cocktail goblet for the chalice. I'll tell you about that later!

From this space a door opened onto the back hall, a long corridor that snaked its way past the "pink" room, the girls' bedroom, made a right turn past the boys' bedroom and then past the kitchen, making a final left turn at the big hall closet, running back past the big bathroom all the way to Mom and Dad's bedroom. The hall was a dark place, lit only by a couple of art deco wall lamps, and made an excellent "fun house" (just like Kennywood Park) when you blocked off the doorways with blankets suspended on ropes tied between the extinguished light fixtures.

Mom and Dad's bedroom was small by this house's standards, but it was ample enough to show off an art nouveau bedroom suite, the high-grain veneer type of furniture I didn't like even as a child. There was plenty of it, too: the head and foot of the bed were great panels; there was a nightstand with a lamp at either side, a huge dresser of drawers, and a great mirror set in a "vanity" for Mom. All this was finished off by a large cedar chest at the foot of the bed. Now this was the one room in the house whose door was sometimes shut (we never knew why), and a place we didn't enter without invitation ("You have no business in that room!"). Funny, I once snuck into that room when I had just made my first communion in second grade. I went to a dish of coins Mom always kept on her dresser and took a nickel to have something to tell in my next confession. I took the nickel, never having stolen anything before in my life, and realized that that was not something I wanted to do. So I put it back.

The boys' room was big enough for ten boys although we only had three at the time. From either side wall a bed came out perpendicularly and still left a very large play space in the middle. We had our own fireplace (outfitted with a gas heater in those days, but strictly forbidden to our touch) and there must have been huge closets somewhere over by the girls' bathroom. Two back windows looked out onto that part of the yard, while another in the corner gave a perfect view of the length of the yard, all the way to Mrs. McBain's garage. This was my corner, with my desk and toy locker blocked off neatly by my twin bed.

Now the boys' room was not always that; it used to be the girls' room, since Bobbi and Maureen were older than myself and Jimmy, in that order. But when Billy was old enough to sleep in a "big" bed, Mom and Dad bought themselves a new Serta Perfect Sleeper with a foam top mattress (we tried it out for days!), and set up the old mattress and box springs on a "Hollywood" frame for the two younger boys, demoting the girls to the other bedroom, only half the size. This was not done without appeasement, however. No, Dad and I got some new paint brushes and a roller (brand new on the market!) and we proceeded to daub the smaller room entirely with an electric pink that no boy could ever sleep in, or really even feel comfortable in it for more than five minutes.

Oh, I should describe the two bathrooms. They were alike in most details except that the one across the hall next to Mom and Dad's bedroom was a good deal longer. They were both completely white: white tile on the walls up to eye level and the plaster wall painted white above that, white built-in tub (no old lion-foot relics here!), sink and commode, the closet and all the woodwork painted white, and white were those wonderful tiny octagonal floor tiles you see in many old bathrooms in Pittsburgh. They were old enough to have settled a bit and provided cracks that formed many interesting patterns for us children to decipher while spending time on the throne. ("Being regular every day is very important! Get into the habit while you are young and you will be happy you did when you get older!")

When we were very little we got the idea (Maureen and I) to experiment with the electric heater in the girls' bathroom. Its electric coils were completely exposed, protected only by a grate with open spaces just large enough to invite trouble. One of us got the idea to see if the coils were hot enough to light some rolled up newspaper. Guess what? They were, and we got a couple of little torches going when Dad came on the scene. He quickly doused the flames in the toilet, then sat down on same (to be at our level) and proceeded to tell us why we were going to be punished. He said, "You have made me very angry with this behavior and I am going to have to punish you. You are never to play with fire! You could burn the house down and hurt yourselves very badly." This was kind of a new RULE, one that I had never heard of, but that was the usual way we learned what THE RULES were anyway. Several whacks with the slipper followed for each perpetrator. Dad had been very afraid for us and the slipper told that tale!

Most of the time being punished was the clear result of some misbehavior, but every once in while I didn't understand why I was being punished, especially by Mom. One thing I could never understand was that when I tried to explain or give an excuse, Mom got mad at me and often told me not to "talk back." To which I promptly replied that I hadn't said anything yet. To which Mom said, "Don't talk back!" To which I ... just rolled my eyes and resigned myself to putting up with a very illogical parent.

The kitchen was elongated by the fifteen-foot extension to each side of the house done in the 1930s. This gave us room on the east end of it for a nice sized breakfast nook with a half-round upholstered bench and a ten-foot closed off pantry behind it. At the other end we had a good sized "mud room" for our myriad shoes, boots, jackets, slickers and an array of hats. That's where the "back door" was, a portal into the small lobby that exited on the side of the house where we entered and exited most of the time. The stove and fridge were on the back wall of the kitchen and the sink looked out to the front street under the shade of a large ginko tree. This beautiful tree was quite unusual in that it dropped all its leaves seemingly in two days each Fall. It also produced a foul-smelling fruit that we had to scoop up in a hurry or the stink made the front porch intolerable. The final element of the house, and not the least important, was this grand front porch that ran the length of the dining room, the foyer and the "good" living room, some fifty-five feet in length. This area was an institution in its own right, and deserves a chapter of its own.

2 – The Family

Now that we have set the stage for our stories, let me now introduce the family, the main characters of this memoir who are the basis of all my memories and of what we believed and what we did back then on Thomas Blvd. I write this memoir to picture how things were back in the 1950s, but I can't help showing a little pride in my family who were always there for me. Our closeness provided a wonderful base of operations in the growth of us all. As I have said, this is not an autobiography, but the family and I are in all the episodes because we are in all the stories I can tell from the inside.

The house was always very alive when we lived there, and there were also other people in the house, the upstairs tenants. Sometimes Schusslers threw candy down from their third-floor sundeck for us kids to chase and enjoy. For several years the Estes put on a first-rate Easter egg hunt for us, with a couple dozen eggs/candies for us to find. We have some old eight millimeter footage of those days, and I delight to stick in a DVD to reminisce and especially to see the many angles of the old house Dad caught on film.

Of the many, many happy times we had, the center of it all was Mom, but I'd better start with Dad, since he was the unquestioned captain of this household. For anything important it was always, "Better ask Dad" or "You'll have to ask Dad for that" or "What does Dad say?" Not that Mom didn't share in major household decisions, and she almost always advocated strongly for the reduction of Dad's punishments, but she always intervened in ways much more subtle than with any open disagreement with "the Head of the Household."

Dad was born in 1918, a denizen of the Homewood section of Pittsburgh, and went to Holy Rosary Church and School. Thus he grew up on the other side of the tracks (the main line of the Pennsylvania Railroad) from our house on Thomas Blvd. Homewood was still quite vigorous in the 1950s, but quite a contrast to the more prosperous Point Breeze, where before they bought a house there, most of the Catholic families got a dispensation to attend church at the more affluent St. Bede or even at Sacred Heart in Shadyside.

I'll have much more to say about Dad later, but for now you should know that Dad was in his thirties when the five of us were kids at 6928. As a teenager in the 1930s Leo Maloney traveled from Homewood by streetcar every day to Central Catholic High School in Oakland. He then graduated from Duquesne University with a B.S. in chemical engineering in 1941 and took a good job with Westinghouse Electric right away. Then he said to his girlfriend Barb (Mom), "Now we can get married." Pretty romantic, huh? Well, he was an engineer! He stayed with Westinghouse until he retired at age 62. And he stayed together with Mom until he passed away in Buffalo at 91 years of age, but that's long after the time we're talking about.

In those days Dad was home for dinner at 5:00 sharp, after which he retired directly to the living room couch (the "old" living room), for TV and naptime. After the eleven o'clock news on TV it was always time for him and Mom for coffee and a snack. He almost always watched a late-night talk show. As for us kids, we never got to talk to him much, except for me when I helped him with his maintenance of the big house. Then, usually on Saturdays, we discussed a lot, and it was a thrill for me to be with Dad doing manly tasks, fetching tools from our cellar workshop, eagerly listening, learning from his disquisitions on how to do just about anything, from the planning and construction of our basement "Rumpus Room," to what kind of car one should buy, to managing real estate—so vast was his practical knowledge that almost no topic could stump him! No subject he discoursed on in those happy hours was ever boring to me!

Dad was always perfectly clear on what was and was not "alahd" (that's Pittsburghese for "permitted") for us kids to do, for he was the author and sole arbiter of THE RULES, a set of unbendable precepts by which our entire childhood was directed until we were well into our teens. To the frequent "No!" response to things that Mom referred us to Dad for permission, there was the following explanatory dictum: "THE RULES are THE RULES!"

Now Mom was the same age as Dad, one of eleven children of an immigrant couple, Croatian and Slovenian, who met in this country, probably at some social event at St. Mary's Slovenian Church on 52nd St. in the Lawrenceville section of Pittsburgh. Mom grew up in the main apartment of their complex of several apartments and storefronts on Butler Street, close to the Allegheny River and a short distance from "dahntahn" ("Center City" for Pittsburghers). After high school Mom went to "business school" for secretarial training, but ended up as a hairdresser, continuing the job she did while going to school. I guess that with four sisters she had learned quite a bit about haute coiffure already at home.

Mom was as easy to please as Dad was not. Her main work was homemaking, so she was always around, cooking up every meal, supervising homework, doing the million household tasks like washing, ironing and housecleaning, so time-consuming back then. Oh, and did she ever supervise how we were dressed ("You're not going to wear that!").

Mom was easy to talk to and listened attentively to all we said. As arbiter of most minor spats—and there were plenty with five of us!—she could end misbehavior with a special pinch under the arm that disabled instantly. It was not often employed, only when reason, shouting, and crying (in that order) didn't work. But Mom knew what we liked: her rich, sweet, bread pudding and warm rice pudding with raisins were to die for, and she knew just the right time to prepare that special evening delight, her pan-fried, sugar-dusted, mouth-watering, apple fritters. Yum!

Our eldest sibling was my sister Bobbi. She was smart, well-liked, and my own personal cross to bear when she hit puberty. I remember being about as big as she was when I was only eleven (she was rather petite). When in her mysterious and frequent frustrations with me she would break a plastic hairbrush over my head or kick me so hard in the shins that I saw stars, I would play the gentleman and never strike back "at a girl." This condescension infuriated her, yet she used it to her advantage many, many times. Before that we were great friends and spent many hours together on the front porch or playing around the house when we were smaller. She was always coming up with ideas, like making a "funhouse" (like "Laughing in the Dark" at Kennywood) in the long back hall, or making an imaginary train out of the dining room chairs all lined up in the foyer. She was responsible for the always delightful and highly competitive bathtub suds competitions between Maureen (with help from Bobbi) in the girls' bathroom and Jimmy and me in the big bathroom on the other side of our bedroom.

Bobbi turned sixteen the summer after we acquired the Bomb, a 1956 Buick Super convertible, with a big V-8 engine. (More on this artefact of my development in its own chapter!) Her friend Mimi Weiser often had use of their family Cadillac, a large dark sedan, and Bobbi's friend Mary Pauline, just across the street, got a new Lincoln Continental convertible for her sixteenth birthday. The three of them liked to drive into Schenley park and race the afternoon away, seeing who could make the best time driving all the way around the oval. Bobbi could hold her own with the Bomb even against the massive engines of the Caddy and Lincoln—people tell me that she can be quite aggressive when she feels the need.

Next is me. My full name is Charles Leo Maloney III, "Buddy" for short within family circles. In school, I was known as "Lee Maloney," a fictitious moniker too much like my Dad's given appellation. I was still "Buddy" at home, but in a logical self-assertion I changed what I was called by schoolmates to "Charlie" when I hit high school. "Brother Elliott" is my religious name, adopted when I entered the novitiate to become a Benedictine monk when I was nineteen. I'm not going to attempt a self-portrait here since this is not, I repeat, an autobiography. That I do appear frequently in the stories is because I'm the one remembering them.

So, let's move on to Maureen. "Reenie" was only a year younger than I, and I guess we were too close in age to be very close. Is there something innate in children that makes them consider it demeaning to hang around with their juniors? The same mechanism makes them always want to be accepted into the company of older kids, even when, most of the time, they are not appreciated. Anyway, Reenie was a pretty girl, quiet, and rather self-sufficient. I think she spent most of her time playing with her dolls and magnificent dollhouse, getting ready, it seems, for raising her four boys later on in Buffalo. It was she, however, who was my chief competition in the bubble bath contests when we were little.

Oh yes, Jimmy was the second Maloney boy, three and a half (light-) years younger than I, and thus considered a non-entity by us older kids, I think, until he got married. He was a happy little boy, and he could sing like a canary. He had his own group of friends and 6928 experiences that I frankly don't know much about.

But I do remember the one time he asserted himself strongly against his bullying older brother. We were battling over the use of a large toy truck. It was his, of course, but as we pushed and pulled in the struggle all he could gain was the tailgate. I taunted him on the useless part of the toy that he had garnered, and that was a big mistake! This was no little plastic toy, it was a right big Tonka Truck fashioned out of real steel. When that tailgate came sailing with a perfect trajectory from the little lefthander straight for the top of my defensively tucked pate, it impacted with a crack that I heard and stars that I saw for the first time in my life. He thus refuted Berkeley in his own childish way. I still carry the evidence of that frontal assault as a cranial dent, now more visible with the passing of years (and hair follicles).

The last to be born into our lives on Thomas Blvd. was Billy, another three and a half years younger than Jim. Billy was the baby of the family until Michael came along some nine years later. But that was in Buffalo and well beyond the timeframe of this story. Billy was born swinging a baseball bat. We have some home movies of him at five years old knocking the stuffing out of every other pitch sent his way by Dad.

Billy was a competitive athlete until he blew out his knee on the baseball field. He can still hit a golf ball 250 yards.

Well, these are the central players in our life at 6928. I hope our stories can help you again touch those wonder years in your lives and help us all remember where we came from and perhaps why we are so complex and yet long for the simplicity we remember (true or not) of those halcyon days.

3 – The Front Porch

I don't think I've ever seen a bigger front porch in Pittsburgh! It rambled at least fifty-five feet long, Dad always maintained, across the full length of the three great rooms at the front of our house, and it was a good fifteen feet deep. The floor was an ocean of narrow tongue-and-groove planks (I'm sure they were oak) painted a flat gray, showing replacement pieces at the front where the rain had done its damage over the years. The ceiling was of tooled wooden slats stained and varnished a warm brown. A single light fixture of colored glass kept sentinel when nobody was home. I guess we never sat out when it was dark.

The length of the porch was divided into three bays with each section marked off by sets of double white Ionic pillars on the front and sides. The center section gave onto a tall stone staircase, almost fifteen feet wide, and punctuated at either side by piers of brick, extending ten feet out from the deck, capped with slabs of the same stone, and topped off with oversize white urns proffering petunias in warm weather. The left and right sections of the porch were guarded front and side by balustrades of white bannisters within a heavy green railing top and bottom.

The floor of each section was accented in season with a woven straw rug of green with white stripes crisscrossing at the borders. We rolled them back every once and a while to sweep up the dust left behind in a lattice pattern that perfectly reduplicated what lay overtop. In the center section there was nothing on the rug to block the way of visitors to the wide front door and its frame of beveled glass, "French" windows, as we called them. On the east end, outside the "good" living room, was the usual porch setting: heavy metal chairs, table, and glider (remember what that is?). All these were painted white and had cloth cushions in yellows and greens, solid colors for the seats and floral patterns on white for the backs. The glider was considered a place for old people (namely, adults) to sit, although we kids could sometimes be seen alone on it, swinging quietly, the faint squeak it made consoling a hurt, and/or beating time to our childish meditations. Here, on rare occasions, I think mainly when Grandma Maloney and our Great Aunt Stella would come, the family sat in conversation with a pitcher of lemonade, or the more usual iced tea, at the ready.

We kids preferred the other end of the porch where a lone wooden swing hung suspended from the ceiling, and we swang on it for hours on end. (Pardon the improper past tense, Mom, I just want to kid you here. [Our Mother would practically kill us if we used bad English!]) The swing was the vantage point from which we watched the cars on the Boulevard and learned to name them, make and model, in animated contests to see who could go the longest without being stumped. I can still name any car from 1954 to 1958 that I see in a movie or at an old car show, make and model. Now how did we judge the contest? Who was the authority? Did we ever bluff? No! We needed no judge because it never entered our minds to cheat at "cars." You either knew the name or didn't, and that was the end of it.

Now you weren't a Pittsburgher if you didn't have a front porch and sit on it for several hours each summer day. I guess we didn't mind the heat so much in those days before air conditioning, and everybody knew that it was much more comfortable outside than in. Most people in town watched the comings and goings of their neighbors from their matchbox porches, but on the Boulevard there were hardly ever any people walking by. This was because there weren't any stores around to walk to, and when people went out in our neighborhood they usually took their car, almost always parked back in the alley in or outside of their garage.

From our vantage point on the porch we would watch the rag man or the fruit huckster ("Ste-rah-beh-ries!"), the knife and scissor sharpener guy, and of course, the ice cream truck pass by. The milkman, the pop delivery man, and the garbage men all used the back of the house which they accessed from the alley. We never saw any door-to-door salesmen, whether for insurance, encyclopedias, or vacuum sweepers. They must have known that in this neighborhood people already had most of their wares, and would never buy them anywhere but at a reputable store!

Boys didn't play with girls much. You had your best friend, your "other" friends, and then the "neighbor kids" (usually a year or so older or younger—anyone else didn't count!) to make up the company that filled up the hours of the summer day. There was one passion I did share with the girls in those days, though, sometimes with just Maureen and Bobbi, but usually with Bobbi and several of her friends, and that was Canasta! We didn't just play Canasta on that front porch, we staged marathons of it, often with two or more tables a-running, or more usually on the floor, with up to six decks of playing cards in a game—never a mere regulation two. This must have been when I was about ten or so; I don't ever remember having much to do with these older girls when they weren't still playing with dolls, that's for sure! Come to think of it, I didn't spend any time with them after this stage either; sometimes they smelled funny.

We loved to sing on that swing, too. All four of us, down to Jimmy, would arrange ourselves on its broad slats and sing "Tell Me Why?" and "They Tried to Tell Us We're Too Young," and try to remember all the words to "Home, Home on the Range." Many happy hours passed by with the four of us not fighting, somehow rendered serene by the cool breeze that always drifted up from under the huge ginko tree at our backs, calmed by being where we should be, on our front porch, in our yard, at our house on Thomas Boulevard.

4 – The Cellar

Wintry and rainy days could never stop us from hours of great fun. We had the mother of all cellars to play in. Its center room corresponded to the large boys' bedroom plus the back hallway on the floor above. It easily accommodated a washer and a dryer, stationary tubs, a mangle, a permanently open ironing board, a folding table (that is, a table for folding the clothes), and shelves for all the supplies for washing and drying the heaps of laundry that swooshed daily down the chute for the Monday wash each week. A little off center was a gas stove standing in the middle of the great space. This was in front of the great pier that held up the whole house with its flue for the basement stove and the fireplaces on each floor above until it emerged out the roof. This pillar also served to fashion a cool skating rink out of the painted red concrete floor around it. The cellar was quite the fun space for us when we were little for two reasons. There was plenty of room for three of four of us to dash round and round the center pillar till we were too tired to play anymore. Second, Mom was usually there amid all the appliances washing or ironing or sorting and folding clothes. I'm thankful for that!

We had a gas dryer, a Hamilton, tolerated only because of the efficiency of natural gas and the fact that Westinghouse did not produce gas dryers. This one had a somewhat faulty pilot light which went out every so often. When that happened the gas automatically shut off, so you had to turn the pilot reset valve back on and relight the gas at the back of the machine. To do that you just rolled a two-foot torch out of newspaper, lit the end, and stuck it through the control panel to the back until the fire caught the gas pilot. A very simple action—until five-year-old Jimmy got the idea to try the process in reverse.

We loved to skate round and round the washroom with our clip-on metal roller skates. You could go slightly downhill from the cellar steps in the other room, whip around the great pillar four or five times on the painted concrete that was as smooth as any roller rink in Pittsburgh, and then shoot off into a third big room that was always completely empty. We never needed to place or store anything there because it was like a foyer (like the one above it) for three more sizeable rooms: Dad's workshop was under the dining room above. There was a storage room jammed to the gills with the train set when not in the exact same spot upstairs in the "good" living room for Christmas, and I-don't-know what all junk in storage. In a third room stood the furnace for the upstairs apartments, with an old coal burning furnace beside it, still operational, that served as our incinerator. Actually, there was a fourth smaller room next to steps to the outside, where the coal must have been dumped in earlier days. More storage room, with a handy toilet when skates made the trip upstairs undesirable.

On one of those uncountable skating days, Maureen and I were racing around in heated competition—Reenie was a very athletic child, and active in sports into her adulthood. We stopped to catch our breath for a moment, and the next thing I knew my pantleg was on fire. To this day I don't know if it was merely by accident that little Jimmy put his reverse gas dryer torch in the vicinity of my cotton pants. All I remember is that they went up very quickly and my first reaction was to flee, on my skates, from the danger, but this only fanned the flames that I could not outrun. Mom heard our screams and with her instinctive ability to interpret the exact degree of distress in a child's cry, she was there in an instant to grab a throw rug and smother the flames.

The burns were fairly serious. I remember bragging about one area of diagnosed "third degree" damage to my left calf which was actually bleeding when Dr. Burke came over to clean and dress the wound. I don't think there existed any pain medication for children in those days—I don't know if there were even any St. Joseph's children's aspirins yet, but that leg hurt and all we had to put on it was butter! After a while everything quieted down but the intense pain of my wound. One of the hours most deeply etched in my memory of those years, however, was of Mom holding me in her lap in the wicker rocking chair. I remember thinking to myself that I was really too big to be splayed out like that over her lap, but as she rocked and calmed me with soothing reassurances that the worst was over, I relaxed a bit and stopped crying. I guess I was eventually able to get to bed that evening, but you know, in spite of the pain, I can't remember a happier moment in my childhood.

When Dad got home there was a serious family meeting that went far beyond any clarification of THE RULES. We were absolutely forbidden to go anywhere near the inside of that dryer. Dad's tone clarified the issue instantly. We never even thought anymore about the gas pilot of that wretched machine!

On another note, Dad's shop was the focus of many happy hours as he and I sawed or threaded or hammered the many items needed to keep such a large house and all its working parts in order. We had a complete set of pipefitting tools, cutters and threaders of every size of those old cast iron pipes that were the electrical and hydraulic nerves of old 6928. We had electrical sockets and switches, wire and tape and conduit, as well as every size of nut and bolt, screw or nail used on the planet, all in jars that cleverly screwed into overhead turntable wheels to dispense them handily. Different kinds of solder, too, were at the ready to be melted down by a blowtorch that must have come from the set of an old Frankenstein movie. It looked like a coffee pot with a spigot and a snout on the top, but it flared out to a fairly precise point when you turned the knob and finally got the flame under control.

In the center of the shop, however, stood our pride and joy, a big electric saw powered by a three-phase, three-quarter horsepower electric motor that we had to wire separately. That baby could easily rip up an eight foot plank or, with a different blade, tailor the most exact crosscuts needed for picture frames or furniture fittings. I was never allowed to do any actual sawing myself and even Dad himself was leery when he used the planer, always using a stick of wood to guide the board. I still remember the lights dimming with Dad's concentration when ripping a big board—or was it the electrical overload of that big motor?

We were very proud of our shop, yet I never remember Dad bragging about it or his terrific ability to fix things, even though it must have saved the family a lot of money. I thought I was very lucky to have a Dad who knew how to do all these things, and it was the joy of my younger days to be working with him on a project so often on a Saturday morning.

Speaking of projects, the pride and joy of Dad's handiwork was the Rumpus Room. This was yet another large basement room, back under the master bedroom and bath on the west side of the house where the cellar steps descended from the side entrance vestibule. First, Dad paneled off those steps, hiding the first floor's furnace and water heater—that baby looked like a small steam locomotive standing straight up on end! He cleverly inserted a large TV (a Westinghouse of course!) into the knotty pine paneling in the area under the landing where the steps made a left turn to descend toward the front of the house. This all left a door-size opening back into the rest of that part of the cellar which became—the Rumpus Room!

To cover the pipes and antique tin ceiling first Dad fashioned a drop ceiling of white pre-acoustical tiles. He covered over the cement floor with a yellow field of vinyl tiles punctuated with evenly spaced blue squares. The side walls, both of large rough-cut limestone since they were parts of the first and then the second foundations of the house, we painted a bright yellow. This kept the area light, along with some fluorescent tubes tucked away in the ceiling tiles. The focus of the entire room was the ten foot bar at the far end. As you entered the space you knew immediately what this place was for.

The bar was Dad's masterpiece. He designed and constructed it himself out of great timbers that smelled fresh when we brought them through the window, for they were far too long to make it down the snaking cellar steps. Actually, I was too little to help much at five years old, but that didn't stop me from relishing the cleverness of my father as I watched the great artefact take shape. He upholstered the broad front with cotton bunting covered with a yellow vinyl skin, patterned with a hundred upholstery nails, a large capital "M" setting off the middle. The bar made a right angle back, giving another six feet to stand at with a lift-up part for the bartender's easy access. There were no stools to obscure its charisma, so you either stood up and leaned on its six-inch machined top edge or you sat at tables placed here and there, ready for cards or an intimate group chat.

The room's most important use was for dancing at my parents' many parties. For this activity Dad purchased a huge old jukebox that he stocked with an array of 78 rpm records: Theresa Brewer, Spike Jones, Nat Cole—all the latest! We inaugurated the room on New Year's Eve of 1951. When the guests arrived at eight o'clock, they were all gathered for the march downstairs to be greeted by a diapered baby Jimmy sashed in white satin with a gold 1951 across his front, complete with party hat and noisemaker which he delighted in sounding. It must have been a great party, but we kids never knew. We were all put to bed—"Children are to be seen but not heard!" you know. How different from friendly gatherings today where the children are so often invited to join the conversation and games until they are dragged off protesting and crying at bedtime.

So that was our cellar. I couldn't count the many fun hours I spent there, and not only on rainy days playing with my brothers and sisters, but also working on some important project with Dad. Of course, we kids had our many, many quarrels and even some pinches and whacks. But we mostly just had a lot of fun with each other. Anger never lasted even to the end of the day when we knelt around the bed in the boys' room to say our prayers together, "God bless Mommy and Daddy," and then all our names in descending order. That sounds kind of over the top—but it wasn't. It's just the way we lived at 6928.

5 – Dad

Dad combed his thick black hair straight back. I always thought that it didn't do much for him, but old photos show that he had chosen the style already in high school. I wonder who told him it looked good that way. Thank God he graduated to a regular parted style by the time we moved to Buffalo! Knowing Dad I don't think he ever asked anyone how he looked, but decided matters of style on his own as he did most things for his whole life.

Dad was always thin for a man considered tall (six feet even) in those days. His build gave him only average power on the softball field, unlike his stardom at bowling, but that was due more to his steely discipline. He told me that his most powerful asset was in his legs, muscle-bound and given to cramps at night, a product of his years of his after-school job, jumping on the foot pedal of the great pressing machine at Aug Schindler's tailor shop and dry cleaners on Race St. in Homewood. You see, after growing up in a rather prosperous household, Dad's life changed radically in 1936.

Dad never told us all the sad circumstances that brought about his need to work long hours to pay for college. We knew that the family had been very well-off owing to their lucrative coal supply business in Lawrenceville, that is, until the St. Patrick's Day flood of 1936 washed the whole concern down the river, coal, trucks, workers' houses and all! Suffice it to say that Dad's father went into a tailspin and Dad had to become the breadwinner for his mother, two sisters and his younger brother who wanted to (and did) become a priest. Grandpa was not a part of our growing up; as a matter of fact, I only remember seeing

Grandpa once. He died when we were very young and I can't remember anything about his funeral.

The Aug Schindler Drycleaners saga, on the other hand, is a long and very interesting one. We never tired of hearing new installments of the story at family gatherings, and we especially liked the old ones we heard before. I guess Aug took quite a liking to Dad and sort of took over as father figure, we might say now, at that critical juncture when Dad was just eighteen years old. Not that Dad ever said a word about all that part, about how important Aug was to him as a young man, he just told about how hard he had to work and then find the time to study in his rigorous engineering program at Duquesne University. Maybe that's why he slept so much every day after work, hitting his favorite spot on a couch in front of the TV where he slept more than watched after dinner.

Anyway, Dad didn't have an imposing athletic figure, but he did enjoy playing softball with guys from work, and he often took me with him when I was about nine or ten. I remember being slightly embarrassed when he would come up to bat only to smack the ball just far enough to reach the outfielder's glove, or--like me later on--just topping the ball sending it down the third base line for an easy throw to first. When he did get on base, however, there was no one faster. Once, when he was rounding third and barreling toward home on somebody else's base hit, I felt terror at the possible collision that might ensue with that big burly catcher, since Dad was stretching his advance in his usual aggressive way at games. I don't remember if he was safe or out, just that he was able to get up and walk away, so that we could join the guys at the bar for one of those great "cold ones" (Coke for me) after the game.

I wonder why I thought so much about this physical aspect of Dad, but I guess every young kid is obsessed with his father's importance and abilities. I was too young to really appreciate his terrific amount of knowledge as an engineer. He really understood things well and from the inside. Later, we would sometimes say, "I would've asked Dad, but I didn't want to know that much about it!"

Well, Dad was quite competitive, as were we all, Mom included. We still play a lot of parlor games at family get togethers, and they are never dull! Once I finally got Maureen's Pictionary clue right, and in her excitement she affirmed my answer by stabbing my hand with the pencil she'd been pointing to the picture with. I think she's a lot like Dad. Once, out at Uncle Johnny's farm at a reunion of Mom's enormous family, the pickup softball game turned into a real contest, with each team taking over the lead every inning. Dad was in left field when a long foul ball came careening out into the weeds. He took off like a rabbit, and with a great leap, shagged the ball to retire the side—only to land on a hidden log which nearly knocked his ankle off as he came down on it. He crumpled down like a rag doll into the rough. The injury was very bad because tears of pain streamed from Dad's eyes all the way to the hospital, with him between sobs urging Mom to drive faster the whole way. It's the first time I ever saw my Dad cry. I understood why he did, but I was not happy with the fact!

The one incident that I regret to have witnessed was when Dad hired someone to wash all the windows of the first floor, to climb up on a ladder, unlock the grills protecting the bedrooms, and after a thorough wash to hook the screens into their slots for summer, and lock up the grills once again. The worker he hired was a black woman named Hazel, a nice person, perhaps with a touch of Graves Disease, because her eyes bulged out noticeably. Anyway, it was a very cool day in May and Hazel told Mom that she was very cold. Mom gave her Dad's old leather pilot's jacket, the kind with all the zippers and flaps. It was Dad's favorite. When Dad came home from work and Mom mentioned the jacket, he was very upset. He frowned and said, "You know that's my favorite jacket. Why did you let her wear it?" With that, Mom said she would send it out to be dry cleaned. Now Dad never spoke badly about black people, and certainly never used the "N" word that was so common at the time, but when the jacket came back from the cleaners, Dad never wore it again. I guess that's just the way things were back then.

At one of my post-game barhops with Dad's softball team the conversation turned to the 1956 presidential election. Dad was giving the merits of the candidate Adlai Stevenson: intelligence, experience, and, above all, he was a real Democrat. (We weren't even allowed to say the word "Republican" in our house!) At the end of his lengthy aretalogy Dad said, "But, of course, I won't vote for him. He's divorced." When I asked him later why his being divorced made Stevenson ineligible, I thought solid-Catholic Dad would say something about it being a sin to divorce and remarry. Instead he said, "If he was not committed to his first wife, how committed would he be to the people who voted for him?"

I know from later conversations with Dad that he was quite the defender of the Catholic faith at these post-game bar conferences and upholder of church regulations. Here's an example: Mom and Dad loved to entertain. They had a bridge club they called the "Egdirbs" (Bridge spelled backwards) and a poker group who called themselves the "Idiots." When their time came to host the party, always on a Saturday night, they provided ample food and drink for the whole evening, except in Lent, of course. Catholics (the faith of least two of the three other couples) had to fast back then, on every day of Lent except Sunday. That meant not eating until midnight. Now that was quite a penance, especially since the non-restraint about drinking made one quite hungry as the evening rolled on. Someone, supposedly some theologian, figured out that the actual time in Pittsburgh, with regard to the precise movement of the sun, was twenty minutes ahead of Eastern Standard Time, and so a fair practice of theirs was to bring out the food at twenty minutes before midnight, easing their hunger, but in full keeping of the law of the church!

One time on a family visit to Buffalo I was telling about a graduate class I was teaching, how we incorporated the teaching of the Second Vatican Council in all our classes in the Seminary. His response was, "Back in the day our Catholic religion was clear and easy to explain. Now, with all this new stuff, I get confused—and I don't like that!" Sorry, Dad, modern theology reflects a more biblical presentation of reality. Besides, life is more complicated than we were taught in the Catechism, if we will admit it. Theology has to continually update itself. We can't believe that the medieval synthesis is the perfect theology, any more than we would want to employ medieval dentistry, and there are a lot of angry Catholics who realize that now.

Such a static approach to the truth was borne out very clearly in our house, however, in its application to the governance of children. Yes, I'm talking about THE RULES. Chores, protocol, expectations, limitations, all were controlled at 6928 by this set of unbendable regulations. No, Dad had never been in the military, an experience Dad was spared because of his high profile job at Westinghouse during World War II. THE RULES were Dad's own idea, a set of unchangeable and clearly articulated restrictions on our behavior, of unknown origin, that were promulgated by Dad to avoid the endless questioning of any seemingly (to children) arbitrary and unevenly applied permissions applied to children whose only logic was what they wanted at the moment. Dad may have been the inspiration of the later quip, "Which part of NO do you not understand?" Instead of an explanation he merely and always answered the most vehement or sob-filled questions with the insuperable dictum "THE RULES ARE THE RULES!"

The first and most unbendable RULE was "Come in when the streetlights come on!" (All THE RULES ended in an exclamation point!) There was actually a seldom-given reason for this RULE, but I think it was more a part of the RULE than an explanation: "There is no reason for a child to be out after the streetlights come on!" Now the tautology of this explanation was lost on us kids, and we therefore dutifully internalized the very sane idea that youngsters are often at risk to themselves and to others if they are away from home after dark. You see, THE RULES weren't all that bad—from an adult perspective. In fact, when we grew up we saw that in the main they make quite good sense, coinciding neatly with what many a city government has tried to accomplish by way of curfews, out-of-bounds areas, and other sanctioned statutes.

The effectiveness of THE RULES was guaranteed in the main by THE SLIPPER. This item of childhood terror was an old (very old, since Dad never got new ones for Christmas from us, or from Mom!) leather-soled bedroom pump that Dad wielded with the dexterity of a tennis champ. He always hit his mark right at the center of one (thankfully clothed) buttock, unless more than three strokes were warranted. In that case an equally expert stroke (or strokes) to the other side ensued. The first one never hurt very much; but oh, those second two! We got the slipper mildly many times, but mostly for infractions of RULE #3 "No running in the house!"

Now, obviously Dad had his nice side most of the time, or I wouldn't be writing about him at such length. Helping him fixit around the house was an irreplaceable source of the deep bond I always had with him till he died. I was with him then. I had just come into the hospital room to relieve one of the nieces on deathwatch when he almost immediately expired. I like to think he was waiting for me, so that Katie wouldn't have to go through the trauma of calling the nurse to verify his passing.

On one occasion in about second grade, I needed a sport coat for some formal event like a family wedding (Uncle Joey's wedding I think). Dad took me all the way downtown to Kaufmann's for this important expenditure. I saw a red one on the rack, and asked Dad if he thought I could have that one. This was not just a sport coat, it was a dress jacket in fire engine red with tiger stripes straight down the length of it. I don't know what got into Dad, but the minute I tried it on Dad loved it, and that was that! I was thrilled that Dad liked it, and I thought I was a movie star! I wore it to church the next Sunday, and oh, did people whisper!

Dad and I also shared yardwork, but there was not much of it even though we had a huge lawn, front and back as well as on the east side of the house. Dad preferred mechanical jobs for his spare time and left the grass mowing to me when I grew old enough. We had a shiny yellow hand propelled reel mower, but when that proved just too much for my eleven-year-old arms, we got a person-propelled gas-powered mower, but Dad strictly forbade me from attempting the steep bank in front of the house. Come to think of it, he was always around when I was cutting, mostly on Saturday mornings in the summer. He was always there, of course, for the Spring fertilizing of the lawn and the Fall leaf burning (at which all the kids helped to gather them into great piles), but they were seldom occurrences in a child's year.

One incident sticks out in my memory: I decided to edge the sidewalk along the front of the house one day, and started out chopping away the sod growing over the cement with an ice chipper. Well, the front of our property was over one hundred feet long, and of course, the sidewalk has two sides (no pun intended). As I moved along I realized that the job was much bigger than I thought. But I kept on edging away, saying, "Well, I'll just do up to the center steps." Then "Well, I'll just go to the end of the property on this side." Then I started the other side and said, "I can make it to the middle today, and finish the rest tomorrow." Then I said, "Well, I guess I should finish the job I've started." This example of working more than was called for (I was about eleven!) is one of the many times I thought it would be good to push myself to do more, just because there was a job to be done. I think people might consider it obsessive-compulsive behavior, but I don't know any successful people who don't suffer from that syndrome at least a little bit! Anyway, I've enjoyed landscaping as a hobby for many a year now, and I look back with joy to those days of hard and sweaty work for a kid, as happy ones. I still get great satisfaction from a neat lawn or garden of my own production.

I'd say that Dad's attempt a "the sex talk" when I was twelve was a disaster. One day he called me into the master bedroom, a place we never entered. He closed the door and sat down on the bed. (I thought I must have murdered somebody!) He then proceeded to tell me about a pleasurable feeling that a boy could have when seed shot out of his penis. This was something that one shouldn't do. I see in my telling of the story that my introduction as an innocent child to the mystery of the begetting of a new human being was really an anti-masturbation warning!

This chapter on Dad was a hard part of this book to write. I hope my decisions of what to include and what to keep private were right, but most of all I hope that fathers of young boys realize that what they do and say in front of their sons is very important and how it impacts their memory and their whole outlook on life.

6 – Mom

Mom! How do I talk about Mom? She was the most wonderful, loving person I ever knew. I guess I'm supposed to be leery of what I might say about Mom, but honestly, I don't think there is an easier person to write about in the whole world. That's just the way Mom was: easy. She was patient and kind; she bore all things, believed all things, hoped all things, and endured all things, as St. Paul tells us about the way love should be. She was like that back then. And when I was a teenager, she used to listen to me for hours as I mused on my religion classes and my philosophy of life. After her long and productive life, it was so hard to see what the stroke did to her, and then her senility. The first time she did not know who I was, I was devastated in ways that I cannot express. She is with the Lord now, her much beloved Lord, just where she should be. But back to then.

Mom's main job in those years was us kids, and she was always home. They tell us that having two parents living at home with the mother always present for the children dropped off radically in the late 1960s, but it was sure nice for us kids to have Mom at home back in the 1950s. It would be wrong to say that we were her whole life, because she enjoyed going out with Dad and especially having people in (at which time we had to disappear!), and she really loved playing cards. Mom was always wonderfully refreshed when she and Dad came back from their vacation in Atlantic City in those early years, and although we could tell that she was really glad to see us, she never fawned on us, protesting such vacuities as, "Oh, I missed you every day." With five of us nestlings constantly cheeping for attention and assistance, I'm sure she was more than glad to get away sometimes. But we always knew we were at the center of all she lived for.

It was Mom who saw to our education and our "proper breeding" (that's what we showed a lack any time we didn't measure up to Mom's strict canons of appearance and polite behavior). Take dinnertime, for example. We had to be on time according to one of THE RULES, as I've mentioned, but it was at Mom's insistence, or at least supervision, that we were immaculately clean, hair neatly combed, and had on a clean shirt (no tee shirts, please!). Dad led the grace, always including "the souls of the faithful departed ... may they rest in peace. Amen." (I often say that prayer for Dad, because he is one of them now.)

After the prayer we all dug in, using knife and fork properly, or having our food nicely cut up for us when we were too little to do it right ourselves. There must have been conversation at table, but I don't remember a single instance of it. What I do remember is that we had to stay at our place until we had finished every morsel on our plate (I forget its number, but this RULE was a biggie!). We might then, and only then, ask "May I please be excused?" (the language was certainly at Mom's insistence).

There were times, however rarely, when Mom had to intervene and either distract Dad or plead for a special dispensation from the "Eat it all!" RULE. One recurrent instance was when had a dinner of turkey soup. Now luckily this didn't happen very often because dinner rarely deviated from the meat-and-potatoes, salad and canned veggies norm. Moreover, people didn't eat turkey all that much in the old days, thank God! But there must have been a RULE, even for Mom, that soup must be manufactured from any remains of either a ham (we ate whole, bone-in, hams back then) or a turkey carcass. The occasional split pea with ham soup was tolerable, but the turkey soup Mom made had a strong and, to our childish palette, overpowering flavor that ruined perfectly good noodles and otherwise tasty bits of turkey–even the heart, which was always the prize. Later, when I was home for a family Christmas party years later, Dad finally did admit that the soup wasn't very good and they never made it anymore.

When we got stuck at table at other times, however, with no reason not to finish our meal other than childish whimsey, Mom was quick to bring up the starving children routine (as the kid in the movie says, "There are children starving in Indiana!"). But Mom didn't just copy all other Catholic moms with words–she had pictures! Remember the little red Missions magazine? Or was it Holy Childhood? The more gruesome the aspect of the diseased children and the more distended their little bellies, the more Mom loved to make us look at the graphic photos!

For Mom Mondays meant washing all day, and Tuesdays were for starching and ironing, mostly on the big "mangle" (Remember those?). Wednesdays were housecleaning. We would fight over who would run the sweeper, because the others had to sweep the kitchen floor, or even dust, ugh! Mom always took care of the kitchen and the bathrooms, however. I guess we could never get them clean enough, but I also think she preserved us from such an odious task because we were such special children (to her). I don't remember what happened Thursdays, but Friday always meant a trip to Kroger's and a heaped-up shopping cart that decanted into at least four shopping bags—no—grocery bags, pressed down, shaken together and overflowing. Supper was always a prepared meal, usually a roast of beef, pork or chicken, always with potatoes (mostly mashed), a can of vegetables heated up and nicely served, and a head lettuce salad which Dad taught us to prepare with Miracle Whip and sugar, yes, a full teaspoon of sugar for every bowl!

When Billy was born, and we other kids were ten, seven, six and three, the work was too much for Mom who was recovering from a Caesarean section birth. Dad agreed to hire our maid, a black woman named Miss Pearl, to help Mom with the chores and to baby sit when Mom needed to rest. Now we liked Miss Pearl, who really loved us kids, and always treated us with the utmost kindness and concern, but we mocked her way of speaking, so strange was it to us children. "Mo' milk, honey" she would ask, and that's all we needed for our taunts: we even called her "Mo' milk," in our half naïve, half snotty way. We never got to know her very well, never even asked if she had children of her own.

When I asked Dad later on how much he had paid her in those days of 1953-54, he told me "Two dollars a day plus carfare (= the cost of a round-trip streetcar ride from her home)." We never asked where she came from.

Mom herself was always a very attractive woman, but Dad says they met at a dance when she went up to him and asked him to show her how to do a dance step he was doing called "the Shag." That is very unlike Mom, who is always very shy and retiring in company, but when Mom wants something it's usually hers in a short time! Mom was always "Mom" and if we ever had the bad manners to refer to Mom as "her" or "she," Mom would promptly intervene with a "Who's 'she'? The cat's mother?"

One of the things I liked best about Mom was how she loved to dress up. She always had nice clothes, nothing too extravagant, but always very smart and complimentary to her fine figure. Children are aware of the curves of a woman's body in a different way from adults, and they certainly know who is good-looking and who isn't. Psychologists have tried to explain what good looks are, I know, and I've read some real laughers of explanations. The fact and the perception of comeliness remain a mystery, but one never lost on even an eight-year-old.

I think Mom always wished she had had the opportunity for a college education. But back then there were no "College for Moms" programs, and it took a lot of time to tend to the five of us (Michael, number six, only came along later when we were already in Buffalo and she was almost forty-four!—there are also good stories from those days!). There wouldn't have been much time for school. I never heard her lament this selfless trade-off, however, or ever talk about it, but she read as much as anyone, some college professors included. Well, nothing ever impeded her from making sure our homework was not only completed as assigned but correct. (Yes, we had homework, and lots of it! We're talking Catholic school here!) I'm sure she didn't actually *do* it for us, any more than any parent should, but she sure did supervise! And Mom was not afraid to talk to us kids about school or whatever else for as long as we needed. She mostly listened to what was on our minds, but when it came to religious questions, Mom really held her own. She always assured us that it was because we were good Catholics that we were so lucky to live so well in the best church in the best country with the best government in the world.

Once Mom shared with me a little lesson on the way God has a hard time with people's pride. One set of upstairs tenants we had were pretty fancy, considering that they rented that huge apartment just for themselves—no kids! It had its own private ingress, a beautifully decorated entrance hall, and a full set of (large) rooms. One autumn they had planned a gala party and had been preparing for a whole week, receiving supplies from a veritable queue of delivery trucks with tables, chairs, crystal punch bowls and goblets—the works! On Friday morning, the day of the great affair, Mom told me all about the pomp and preparations and how God sometimes lets us know we are not all that we might think we are. She took me over the window and pointed out to the street. There would be no elegant egress to a line of fancy cars and limousines that night, for along the curb of the entire front of our property were heaped in enormous piles all the leaves the city workers had collected from the whole block–and left for the weekend to be picked up on Monday following!

Since Grandma spoke with a strong accent, Mother decided she would have none of that. And she was a tyrant over us in the one area of linguistic perfection. Mom spoke perfect English, better than Dad's old fashioned, "Again I go to the store it'll be three o'clock," and "Supposn' it was already three o'clock...." Oh, we had to use only the correct forms. And I mean perfectly! We were corrected at the slightest mispronunciation or grammatical hesitation. Unspeakable atrocities like the Pittsburger "y'ins" were anathema in our house, and we looked down on anybody who used them. "Ain't" and similar colloquialisms were as unthinkable as "swear" words.

Any vulgarity whatsoever was unthinkable because of Mom. "Hell" and "damn" were as out of place as the worst blasphemies, although their surrogates "heck" and "darn it" were acceptable—barely—only if used sparingly. Once I woke up in the middle of the night (we were always in bed at nine on weekdays—RULE #5). I heard Dad trying to readjust the huge exhaust fan in the dining room window. I was still in the hall by the foyer when the fixture must have slipped and smashed his fingers pretty painfully, for he said, "Son of a bitch! Bastard!" I spent many hours trying to reconcile this (private) lapse of morality in my father, never fully resolving the issue until I was a young adult and had some worse slips in my own language!

Whenever we hurt ourselves or when Lent started getting us down (no candy or movies!) Mom always told us to "offer it up for the poor souls in Purgatory," a practice that still helps me today. You see, when you pray about it, you name what is bothering you and you don't have to misdirect any energy into fruitless denial or worse. It has also, I believe, been responsible for the complete clearance of that site of postmortem penance, or so I have told my friendly dentist on several occasions when I was on the business end of his instruments of remediation.

Mom would also listen to the Jehovah's Witnesses for hours when they came to the door. When I asked her why she would put up with their harangues, she said that she felt sorry for them since they didn't seem to have much of a life, and she knew that they would feel better if they could preach for a while. Mom was absolutely solid in her oldtime Catholic faith, and yet she was the first to accept wholeheartedly the changes of Vatican II because they were made officially by Church authority. Secondarily, she saw that most of them were pretty good!

Mom also talked about religion with a young woman named Inez, who lived for a while in the studio apartment above our kitchen. (Actually, it was a studio with a kitchen and a full bath—and Mom promised that I could have it when I would reach high school age!) Anyway, Inez was a Mormon, and Mom shared with me one day her complete puzzlement at a question Inez had asked. If she, Inez, were willing to give up her belief and become a Catholic, she had queried, would Mom then agree to become a Mormon? On the unthinkable, Mom could only say, "Can you imagine that?!" No, Mom, I don't think so.

Mom and I would sometimes spend time together dreaming of renovating the whole house. We would gradually move the second-floor tenants out and then reconstruct the front staircase down into our large foyer in its original splendor. It would go through the girls' bedroom, turning a one-eighty-degree bend on a landing, and lead to the great upstairs living room (it was the size of our living rooms and foyer combined!) which would become a grand ballroom. We would have guest quarters with its own private entrance, and every last one of us could have our own bedroom! Take your pick of the three downstairs, three more upstairs. I don't know what we were going to do with its huge dining room, kitchen and breakfast sunroom, not to mention the three rooms on the third floor, and don't forget my studio apartment! So many hours we passed in happy conversation, and even more when I was in high school! God bless you, Mom. I sure miss you!

7 – Christmas

The house stayed pretty much the same throughout the year except for the one time when the whole order of things was upended in happy confusion: Christmas! Elaborate preparations for this joyous time of the year began a whole week before the Twenty-Fifth, with the annual search for just the right Christmas tree. This had to be a large (about eight foot) long-needled pine that was put into its water-filled stand to shed its magic aroma all through the house for a full two weeks and more.

We decorated for Christmas each year with much checking of burned out tree lights, often replacing them with a new set, but always using the old candlelight set, whose upright cylinders formed candles filled with colored water that actually boiled up from the heat of the lamp and bubbled with great effect on the tinsel-strewn branches. We had many old ornaments, bulbs of various bright colors, and candy canes that we would pilfer from the tree and suck on every day after our stockings' supply of candy ran out. The tinseling of the tree was highly supervised by Mom who wouldn't let us just throw the stuff in clumps on the tree, but made us place a few strands neatly on the end of a branch, careful to let it drop straight down, not bending or covering another ornament. On top, we had a Christmas star, bigger and more prominent than any other ornament, shining out brightly through its plastic rays, to announce the true meaning of Christmas to be found underneath the tree in our traditional Nativity set. The Holy Family were centered round the manger with an angel hovering somewhere overhead. We had Wise Men and shepherds, sheep, cows and camels, the whole set, but no Little Drummer Boy.

Next came the oversized train set that took up half the room in front of the tree and the fireplace, extending almost the length of it. This Christmas-only artefact started out with a four by six-foot platform and Dad's childhood Lionel O Gauge train set, but was soon expanded by the addition of another platform, this one an eight by four foot board with a trestle that ran around the perimeter and a figure eight that you could switch the track to in the middle. Working on all of this down in Dad's workshop is my first memory of Christmas. I remember fondly how we ran that train for hours on those happy, school-less days before New Year's.

We were not "alahd" (= "permitted") to open gifts until Mom and Dad joined us early risers on Christmas morning. Needless to say, there was no peace for them until they arrived on scene. I got a sled one year, a Flexible Flyer that I steered right into a tree over in Westinghouse Park the next day. A year later we three older kids got bikes, I, my twenty-four-inch Higgins red street bike that I just about wore out in those years, riding like a demon all over Point Breeze. Maureen got a green girls' bike, you know, with the lowered middle bar that you could step through. Bobbi got the prize, being older. She got a blue Schwinn "English racer," as we called them back then, with five gears to choose from!

There was candy in each stocking and wonderful cakes and cookies for every meal. I don't remember anyone ever being disappointed with their gifts from Santa. After all, we did go all the way downtown to Kaufmann's and told Santa ourselves what we wanted! We all know that "It is better to give than to receive," but it sure is wonderful to be a kid when you get something nice for Christmas!

Maureen tells me she always got a new dress for Christmas, and was thrilled to have it, even when it sometimes was a hand-me-down from Bobbi (not too often) that she grew into. She got a cook set one year which she loved. "I played my heart out with it," she told me. Oh, and a walking doll one year, too, whatever that is. Girl stuff.

We had the Maloney side uncles and aunts over with all our cousins for dinner every Christmas Day. Cousin Marilyn tells me that they loved to come to our house because it was so big. "There were all kinds of places to explore, to run and play, upstairs and downstairs, inside and outside of the house. We could even play hide-and-seek inside!"

When Christmastime was over, we were all sad to unceremoniously take the tree down, now sere and dropping its long needles all over the place. Cleanup was a major family project with Dad detailing every part of it to perfection, and the "good" living room was back on its interdiction for all minors until that blessed time should roll around the next year. Christmas is one event for a child that is certainly made better by a modicum of prosperity. Hate to say it, but it's true.

8 – Family Activities

Birthday parties were important when we were little. We'd have our neighborhood friends over for cake and ice cream, performing all the necessary rites with candles, singing "Happy Birthday," making a wish and blowing them out. I can't remember what I wished for, for the life of me! I honestly don't remember ever needing anything very much and there were plenty of happy events to fill up my young life with sufficient happiness, I'd say, week by week. There was often a birthday family meal at Poli's in Squirrel Hill. We all looked forward to that treat where we all ordered their delicious, huge, fried shrimp.

There was the Willows swimming pool (in Verona, I think) where we went, it seems, for the whole day in summer. The Blue Dell Motel swimming pool was just as nice, but not as much fun, because coming back from the Willows we always stopped at Eat 'n' Park where we each got a "Big Boy" hamburger and fries, and, oh, in season the strawberry pie was to die for!

Of course in summer there was the great adventure for me and my friends called Frick Park, a short bike ride away. I don't think there was a salamander in the park that we hadn't found and put back for another day. Little League didn't interest me much after one season, probably because no one on the staff seemed very interested in me. I don't know where Dad was in all of this, but other than an occasional game of "catch," he didn't spend any time on b-ball with me. I guess that by the time I was old enough to play my two younger brothers took up a lot of time and energy, so I never got the parental teaching on throwing the ball and playing the game. We listened to the Pirates baseball games a lot, but hardly ever tuned in to the woebegone Steelers in those days.

But for my gang football was a different story. My friends and I all had full equipment: shoulder pads, padded pants, and helmet with faceguard, and we loved to crash into each other, always playing tackle ball—it only took seven or eight of us to make a game. There wasn't very much to learn for ten and eleven-year-olds other than the basic rules of the game, which were quite simple back then: center the ball to the quarterback and knock the heck out of each other until the ball carrier was down.

I've already mentioned the antics of Nicky and me playing a variety of mortal combat games over yards and atop garage roofs, or in the hills and woods nearby in some neighborhood lots. There were swings and climbing bars in Westinghouse Park nearby, but when we were little we already had our own "Jungle Gym" in the side yard in front of the garage.

We played "Fish" and "Crazy Eights" a lot before we graduated to the canasta marathons we loved so much. Mom and Dad's great enthusiasm for the game of Bridge came through to us, for whom it became mandatory to learn all the proper opening bids and first responses, the rudiments of playing of a hand, and even a slam convention or two. All this by the time we were ten, so that we could play an enjoyable game with Mom and ourselves, even though there was an awful lot of crossboarding and changing of bids. This, of course, is strictly verboten in Bridge—but we were ten and twelve!

Now as for television, we had one and we enjoyed it! Very early on, as we've seen, we got a Westinghouse TV at a very good price. I believe it had an 16 inch screen, which was quite viewable from the distance people said it was necessary to view at for safety's sake, lest the rays or something hurt your vision. Anyway, Howdy Doody began on TV in the late 1940s, and I remember watching the show as early as 1952. I was an avid viewer for years, and I have to say that as that last show in 1960 drew to a close, I knew that Clarabell would say something after all those years of silent miming and squeaking his horn! Do you know that the original Clarabell became Captain Kangaroo after he left the show in 1952?

Saturday morning kids' shows were a must, from cartoons like Mighty Mouse to the "Adventures of Sky King" when we got a bit older. Captain Video was "on" at 7:00 PM Monday through Friday, but this conflicted with the rosary which played on the radio, also at 7:00. We knelt at the dining room chairs we turned around every evening then to say the rosary with the radio, and then scurried into the living room to try to catch up with the exploits of the Captain Video program already in progress. The "Superman" show, starring George Reeves, started in 1952, and I think we watched every episode until it concluded in sometime in 1958. Finally, everybody knows when the Ed Sullivan show was on. Every Sunday evening at from 8:00 to 9:00 PM, I think everyone I knew must have watched every show to see what new talent he would have on: Elvis, the Beatles, along with the great entertainers of the day like the ventriloquists Señor Wences and Edgar Bergan, or a new routine by Abbot and Costello or Dean Martin and Jerry Lewis. I think it truly was the golden age of television!

There was quite a bit of family activity that centered around church and our attendance at the many services and functions that took place at that sacred venue. School, of course, and its many-faceted involvement of parent and child alike also has a whole section of its own. We'll save those for the last in Parts 3 and 4 of our book.

9 – The Bomb

Now Dad liked his cars! He was able to pick up, in 1951, a 1950, two-door Buick Super, not a pretty thing, all off-white green with a blue top, but for its day, the car could move! This is the earliest car of ours that I can remember, often parked at the ready, not in the garage but on Thomas right in front of the staircase up to our front yard.

In late 1955, after our friend George McGannon had sported his brand new Buick (a two-tone light green and white Roadmaster convertible—quite a car!) for almost a year, Dad could stand it no longer. He ordered up from the factory exactly what he wanted: a two-toned 1956 deep pink (they called it "coral") and black Buick Super convertible, with a white top and two-toned black and white leather seats—the Bomb!

We called it "the Bomb" for two reasons. When we got it in October of 1955 there was nothing like it in the neighborhood. It made quite a statement with its size, its newness, and its colors. And second, it could fly! When you "floored it," the Dynamo transmission "switched its pitch" and it roared, seemingly standing the car up on its back tires which squealed and "laid rubber" like a racecar.

This was no ordinary car. It had the full-sized body and roomy interior (four holes along the side—remember?) but not all the luxury of the Roadmaster. Dad had thought about this purchase thoroughly. There were four models of Buicks in those years. The Special was out of the question. You see, the Special had the smaller body and a small engine—it may not even have been a V-8! That would make people wonder why you bought a Buick in the first place: "If you can't afford a proper Buick, then buy a Pontiac!"

The Century, I'm sure, caused Dad no small distraction. It was the hotrod of the line, for although it shared the smaller body with the Special, it had the big 255 horsepower engine. While both the Super and the Roadmaster had the big engine with the larger frame, the Roadmaster was rather more expensive, and it made the statement, "This is the biggest and the best!" Dad was a humble man for all his knowledge and acuity, and after all we wouldn't want people to say, "Who does he think he is, George McGannon?!

Actually, the entire range of automobiles in that day had a distinct hierarchy and message to proclaim about the owner. Take General Motors cars, for example. The Chevy was a good reliable car. Nobody in our neighborhood drove one except Grace, Sheedys' maid, but there were plenty of them parked along the streets down in Homewood. The Pontiac said that you weren't poor, but striving either to get a better job or keeping your parents from worrying too much. An Oldsmobile was a nice car, but Pittsburghers preferred Buicks two to one. Buick announced success while Cadillac…. Well, it was the Cadillac of cars, wasn't it?

Take Sheedys, for example. Everybody knew they had money. After all, Doctor Sheedy was a physician, and a specialist at that. They even had a white maid! Their cars were a Cadillac for the doctor and a great, beautiful 1953 blue Buick convertible for Mrs. Their son Pat and his sister ran around in a cream colored 1954 Pontiac, a pretty nice ride for a couple of teenagers. But when Dr. Sheedy bought an end-of-the-line 1955 Cadillac when the new models came out in 1956, he caused quite a stir in the neighborhood.

I suppose you might wonder where I learned all this lore about cars. Well, Dad and I didn't talk a lot when I was nine, except on those long afternoons when we were fixing something around the house. Dad did almost all of his own maintenance work on the big old house. After all, the thing had eight large and larger rooms and two full baths on the first floor. There were some nine rooms in the second-floor apartment, including a lower and an upper entrance lobby. Another four rooms made up the apartment on the third floor, along with the attic and the studio apartment with kitchenette and bath. The basement had a total of nine rooms of its own. While I assisted in these jobs, often fetching "a crescent wrench" or a "compass saw" from the workshop in the basement, Dad would expound at length on subjects that it was important for a young boy to know about. Yes, there was a complete etiquette for what car you drove, and it was a good thing to keep in mind on any occasion.

My sister Bobbi turned sixteen the summer after we got the Bomb. I've already mentioned how she could hold her with her friends' Cadillac and Lincoln in their Schenley Park racing. I only got to drive the magic vehicle when I was sixteen, and I almost finished it off through my inexperience. Yes, I wrecked the car, but I won't tell you about it here because it happened in Buffalo, very much outside the parameters of what we're telling in this book. Suffice it to say that Dad took the whole event very Stoically, and I even learned how he actually did care for this teenager in his genuine concern for my safety.

You may wonder why I tell about the family car so early in this story. Do I still live in that American myth that your car defined you and your goals? No, but in those days that car did give us a certain pride, and just as the house was so special, the Bomb conferred a certain dignity on our family; it spoke in some way something of what we thought of ourselves. This is best illustrated by a spontaneous answer from me to one of the older girls in the neighborhood. One day when Dad asked me to put the convertible top down for the afternoon, to get ready for a Sunday drive, Martie came up behind and said, "Really, Buddy, don't you think this car is a little too flashy?" "It may be too flashy for your family," I shot back, "but it's not too flashy for ours!"

Part 2 – The Neighborhood

1 – Friends

There were several boys around my age in the neighborhood, almost all of whom I knew and had some interactions with on and off in my early years, but my best friend was Nicky Criss. I probably played with four or five friends who lived within a hundred yards of our house, but Nicky was the special one. Nicky was not quite a year older than I and lived across the alley on Meade St. with his parents, his younger brother Russ and little sister Sally. He was tall and skinny; he was smart and liked adventure as much as I (he ended up flying F-5 Tiger jet fighters in Viet Nam!). We spent an incredible amount of time together, probably most of the day every free day when we were little, roaming the alley, playing army or "cowboys and Indians" with play guns and realistic death scenes. We built shanties in our back yard, scavenging wood from the old mansions that were continually being torn down in Point Breeze in those years. What a sad end to so many magnificent edifices—later including 6928! But we didn't care then, and they were a great source of all kinds of wood, even a door or a window when needed. We rode our bikes in the alley and on the streets all around our little neighborhood in North Point Breeze, even across Thomas over and into Westinghouse Park. But when we went up to the Fire Station and McCarthy's Drugstore, or further to Frick Park, we stayed only on the sidewalks of those busy streets.

Nicky's family was Protestant (actually Presbyterian, but all Protestants were the same to us then—they weren't Catholic!) and so we got split up when we started school, he going to Sterrett School, the local public institute up on Reynolds Street where I went to Kindergarten. I, of course, went to Holy Rosary down in Homewood. But that didn't change this buddy system. There were still lots of weekend games and all summer, too, for bikes and some mildly hazardous escapades, but we'll save that for later.

A very special event that I shared with Nicky for several years was the annual Memorial Day Parade. We worked for some time weaving red-white-and-blue crepe paper through the spokes of our wheels, wrapping the handlebars with it, and sporting American flags flying from antenna-like rods attached to the rear axle. We would join in with all the other kids on bikes who trailed the parade after the bands and troops of scouts, vets, Lions, Elks and all passed by. Then up Dallas Avenue (in the middle of the street!) all the way to Homewood Cemetery, where a Memorial ceremony took place. We never stayed for the services, however; they were only a bunch of boring speeches.

One of our special places to roam in was Frick Park, and I'll bet that by the time we were twelve we knew every salamander there by name! We played Little League baseball at the Frick Park ballfields over on Forbes Ave. and even dared to go down into Fern Hollow at the extreme end of the park, just to see what we could see. We did all kinds of exploring together, including what our bodies were like and how they reacted at about the age of seven or eight. Funny how that phase started out of the blue and concluded just as quickly. A couple of years later, we were old enough to jump on a streetcar (for a dime!) and go to the Carnegie Science Museum together. All Pittsburgh children must have been as thrilled as we were to go to the dinosaur room and imagine perilous scenes of narrow escape from the jaws of that big T-Rex. Steven Speilberg surely had home movies of our imaginations when he created Jurassic Park!

Our friendship held fast even when Nicky's family moved to a quiet little neighborhood above Frick Park. In fact, the change may even have improved our link since we started playing football and sled-riding at the large field behind Shadyside Academy up there on Braddock Avenue. This venue was very near Nicky's house, and I often got to spend an overnight there, especially as winter came on, when the streetlights were on so early. Nicky and Russ had the whole third floor of their house all to themselves, and there we spent many hours yakking away into the night or reading Popular Mechanics and the like on rainy days.

It was the drastic move to Buffalo that changed everything. I visited Nicky once or twice afterward when we would come to Pittsburgh, but adolescence blurred former ties as it did everything else, as new relationships crowded into our lives. I saw Nicky only once again, many years later when I made it a point to visit him in San Diego when I was out there at a biblical conference. Nicky was a wonderful friend. He was a good, honest and interesting boy who deserves more than thanks can say for all the good times, and even the sad. We managed to get into trouble together more than once! I wonder if I'd still have a deep, dark secret if he hadn't cracked under parental pressure and told that it was the two of us who scratched up Grace's Chevrolet. And, you know, he never tried to put the (deserved) blame on me alone! It was a simple escapade gone wrong, but it deserves its own telling after we introduce my other friends. How odd it seems to me that neither of us, who had shared so much precious time together, succeeded in connecting again until one visit and a few letters almost four decades later. But when his brother Russell died suddenly at a young sixty years of age, Nicky called me to meet Russ' family and lead a prayer at the Pittsburgh funeral home.

Denny Sheedy was younger than I but older than my brother Jimmy, and I guess Bobbi was more "friends" with his sister Martie. Anyway, we spent time with Denny and he was a lot of fun. When he was about six he got a big cowboy hat and a silver sixgun set for Christmas. He loved that outfit and wore it so often that everybody started calling him "Hoppy," after Hopalong Cassidy, the "Must-See-TV" cowboy program of our childhood. Denny was a likable kid who had a big boxer dog called "Baron," but you never saw Denny playing with Baron or walking him on a leash. For Baron was "king of the streets," as we used to say, and quite independently roamed all around the neighborhood terrorizing all other dogs. One day he met his match and returned home all torn up and bleeding badly. After that he was kept in Sheedys' newly fenced-in backyard to avoid further mishap.

One boy, Doug (can't remember the last name) who lived in one of the big houses on Meade Street met up with me on bikes in the Alley when they moved in about this time. On a rainy day we were playing upstairs in their house when I went to find a bathroom. When I turned the corner to enter one door I was presented with the completely nude figure of their babysitter toweling off from a shower she had just taken, having entered from another room. She screamed, I ran, and hoped that that encounter had never happened. Later that evening Mr. What's-Their-Name came to see Dad, who received him in the good living room. That meant it was serious. When he left Dad called me and interrogated my side of the story. When I told him that the episode was completely unplanned by me who did not know the house nor even that they had a nanny, Dad accepted the truth as the truth and that was the end of the matter. I didn't even get any advice because, really, there was nothing to say. Not sure why, but I never spent any time with Doug after that.

At the end of our alley, across Murtland, lived Stan Hahn. I first noticed Stan in the vacuum created by Nicky's departure, and I instantly liked him when I talked to him, even though he was a year or so younger. He was a nice looking boy whose family owned Hahn's Furniture Stores, and they lived at the end of our alley in a magnificent house on Murtland Ave. They were Jewish, or at least the Dad was, but as with Nicky, we never talked about religion or even where we went to worship. Somehow we were all oriented at home not to bring up such a touchy subject. But why was it considered touchy?

Stan and I spent a good deal of time together, but instead of roaming around all over the neighborhood "doing things" as Nicky and I always had done, we usually stayed around his house, deep in conversation for hours at a time. Funny, I can't remember a single thing we talked about. He was the only boy from the old neighborhood I visited consistently after we moved away. In fact, it is true to say that our liking for each other only grew stronger with the passing of time, I suspect because of the onset of puberty and the beginning of those powerful feelings of attraction between young friends. It's all different, isn't it, when you start to care about someone and what they think of you, and whether they like you and are proud of your friendship in the company of others?

Interactions escalate, too. I was a bit older, as I've said, and was growing up faster than Stan. One day I tried to show him a "judo flip" I thought I had learned watching TV wrestling. Whether I did it correctly or not, I don't know, but Stan went down and landed so hard that he couldn't hold back some pain-induced tears. He was very embarassed and I walked away to another part of the yard to let him recover from the shame of actually crying in front of another kid. As I was bent over, engrossed in some occurrence among the insects in a flower bed, Stan came up behind me and let go with a kick. Now it wasn't on purpose, I know, but it was forceful, and it caught me below the intended buttocks, right in the testicles. Wow, did I see stars!

After I recovered a bit I ran after him, threw him down hard, and then stormed out of the yard—in total confusion. I had just deliberately offended (and hurt again!) my really good friend, having been out of control of myself for perhaps the second time in my life. What a shame I was unable to concede that his mistaken blow was as painful as my inept judo maneuver had been, and the both of us shake it off, forget it, and pick up where we left off before it all began. But much more than the pain, more than the idea that a smaller kid had really gotten the better of me, I had been truly nonplussed at how my feelings had been hurt by such retaliation. I had no response at my disposal other than to strike out and quickly disappear from the scene in a frenzy of pain, now more emotional than physical.

The incident was over and forgotten in a day or so and we were back at being friends right away. The Hahns had a huge side yard that furnished the field for a neighborhood football game every Saturday. Now this was serious football, tackle, not touch, and all the boys in the neighborhood from ten to sixteen took part in them. In fact, it was there that I met and got to know many of the older boys who lived on Meade St. and even the next block of Thomas. My older sister always asked me about them after the game. Girls!

Gradually, of course, time and distance eroded my friendship with Stan, and we fell out of touch by the time I went to college and entered the monastery, yet I was deeply shocked when I heard about his sudden death with his new wife in a car accident on their honeymoon on Cape Cod. I had been in Rome, studying, and heard of his death in the most awkward way. You see, when I returned to the Abbey one summer, I decided to call Stan to see what was up. The maid answered the phone and I asked to please speak with Stan. She got quite flustered and said, "You'd better speak to Her!" Mrs. Hahn took the phone and told me about Stan's tragic death. What could I say? I quickly explained that I'd been out of the country, in Italy, and hadn't heard. I gave my condolences and quickly got off the phone with nothing more to say.

I think it was the Spring of 1959, just before we moved to Buffalo, that I first took any real interest in girls. I had just turned thirteen and was still a child physically. I know this for a fact, because the doctor who examined me for my entrance into high school seminary wrote that down on my report. When I asked him what "somewhat immature" meant, he said that for my age I should have more hair on my body. That really helped my self-image, I can tell you! Well, that all changed quickly. The very next year, after riding home on the bus with the guys from a school basketball game, and observing some horsing around in the back of the bus with poor James T. who was being depantsed and taunted because he was still immature at fifteen, I experienced the first stirrings of puberty. But all that came later than we're telling about in this book.

Now down our alley and just across Dallas Avenue lived Ginny Morgan. She was a very smart girl who played their "baby grand" piano very well. She studied and read all the time, later to become a high school French teacher. Her Dad was very Protestant, at least that's how I interpreted his severity, a prosperous dentist with offices downtown in the Jenkins Arcade. Mrs. Morgan, however, was Catholic, and so Ginny was "raised a Catholic." Although she went to Sterrett for elementary school, she would go with her best friend Donna Pugliano to Sacred Heart High School in Shadyside the next year. The two girls had connecting backyards behind the corner of Dallas and the 6800 block of Thomas, the block that had the islands of cherry trees down the middle that were supposed to remind one of Paris, we were told. Donna was a very pretty girl with a cute figure as I remember just starting to notice that kind of thing.

I don't know how we got started spending time together, but I remember how very nice they were to me, always having time when I did, and always baking me my favorite chocolate cake or cherry pie. Now these two I did visit when I came to Pittsburgh every Christmas and Eastertime for the Camp Rosary reunions in the following years. They were good and constant friends, especially Ginny whom I still visited from time to time until she moved away from the old neighborhood. On my Burgh visits I would almost always make time to join her at the piano and sing some pop hits before we had a bite of my favorite pie or cake while I told of my aspirations in the seminary.

I was friends with Mark McNally about the time we were planning to move to Buffalo. He spent some time with Stan Hahn and me until one day I caught him torturing my little brother Jimmy, teasing him by calling him names. I took exception to this, up at Meade Place by the two stone rooks that were left there from the Heinz mansion. I wrestled him down to the ground, pinned his shoulders against the sidewalk, and threatened more harm if he did not stop taunting my brother. This he did, and we didn't see much of each other again, but then we moved away to Buffalo a month later. Sixty-five years later we had a pleasant lunch at the Point Brugge Restaurant on Reynolds St. where Mark recalled that "dust-up," as he called it. We talked for two hours and remembered so many things as if they had happened yesterday! The "dust-up" was a very rare occurrence for me, who had never, and have not yet, ever struck someone with a fist to the face. Thinking about the incident makes me wonder at how quickly violence becomes the option when family honor or safety is at stake.

Speaking of violence, there was one incident of it that puzzled me greatly. We were playing football in Westinghouse Park, some kids from

Holy Rosary, including Richie and Alan, the Sauerwein brothers. (We Pittsburgh-ized that fine German name into something like SAHR-wine). During the game I had some difference of opinion over a call with a tough kid from Homewood called Tommy. (No, this was not good-hearted Tommy O'Malley whom we'll meet in another story.) When the tough Tommy said, "Step across this line," (which he drew on the ground with his foot), I playfully crossed it laughing and saying, "Now what are you going to do?" Well, he hauled off and sucker punched me right over my left eye—as hard as he could! It didn't knock me down but it hurt badly. My immediate reaction was to say to myself, "Now why would one boy do that to another?" As I've said, I've never tried to punch anyone in the face in my life, and I certainly was not going to try to retaliate against that tough boy. He was quite a bit heftier than me, and I knew he was street-smart, too. Uh-uh, that would be a lose-lose! Besides, we were just not fighters in our group. We never needed to. Since we didn't fight, we didn't know how! So I just moved on back to huddle with my team, pretending that nothing had happened. When the contusion swelled up so big that I could actually see the bulge with my left eye, he came over and said something smart like, "I really got you good, didn't I?" I just said, "Oh this? This must have happened when I bashed into Richie on the last tackle." I had never counted this Tommy as a friend before this football game. And I certainly didn't after it!

2 – The Alley

The city block we lived on was sliced in two by a service road to the back of our homes on the 6900 block of Thomas, so deep were the lots that we all had garages behind our houses, accessed from this alley. It thus also backed Meade St., the next street south, below Penn Ave. Formally it was called Lark Way, but never by us. We just called it, "The Alley." It was on this surface that we all learned to ride our bikes, even as it was the social center of our neighborhood for us kids who lived in the stately homes on Thomas and the various dwellings on Meade St. The lengths of Murtland and Dallas Aves. at the ends of the Alley completed the locale. Much of population, the Criss family, the Sheedys, Mortons, Waddells, Smiths, Hahns, and McNallys all had kids of various ages for the five of us Maloneys to play with.

As you entered the Alley from either end there was a big yellow sign that said "Watch Children." It ruffled my feathers every time I passed it. I read it as "Watch! Children," speaking directly to us youngsters. I don't know how many times I thought, "Don't tell us kids to 'Watch!' it's the adults who should watch out for us!"

It was usual for both Dad and Mom to park the car here in the Alley. On many a sunny Saturday afternoon Dad and I would wash the Bomb, listening attentively to the Pirates' game on KDKA with Bob Prince announcing. After winning a particularly close game, he would always say, "We had 'em all the way!" At least once a season we would wax the car, the old way, rubbing the wax on in patches and when it dried, taking another soft cloth to "buff it up" to a shiny finish.

Here Nicky and I played soldiers or cowboys and Indians for hours, running and hiding and shooting our cap guns and play rifles. But it was in our back yard, never out into the neighborhood, where we played hide-and-seek. This was never a pastime for the neighborhood boys, but we Maloney sibs played it together, all of us but Billy who was too little, so many, many summer afternoons when we weren't swinging and hanging from the jungle gym behind the garage.

I can still see myself careening down Murtland St. making the turn into the alley, no hands, with just my knees and body torque maneuvering that red Higgins into the turn. I lived on that freedom provider for a couple of summers back then. I'd just hang my football helmet on the handlebars and head up to Nicky's Shadyside Academy field, for many an afternoon of full contact, tackle football with whatever kids were out playing from his neighborhood. Never a fear, never a worry about coming home from that distance, just a lot of care crossing Penn Ave.

Once, riding down Homewood Ave. I flew out from the sidewalk between two parked cars to ride home over Meade St. I didn't see the oncoming convertible over the parked cars and shot right out into the street in front of the unsuspecting motorist. He slammed on the brakes—I remember the car skidding sideways. He was very upset and yelled at me, asking where I lived. I was so afraid he was going to tell my parents and I'd get into trouble. After a minute or two he calmed down and yelled, "Be careful, kid! We could'a had a terrible accident!" He drove away, trembling I'm sure, just thinking of what it would be like to have been going a little too fast and striking a kid like me on a bike. Thank you, God, for both of us that day!

3 – McGannons

The McGannon boys were an exception to the proximity of my earliest friends: they lived on the 7100 block of Thomas, at the great distance of two blocks away. The origin of our acquaintance was not, therefore, the inevitable encounter in our alley as with the rest of the gang, but it happened that their dad and mine were high school buddies at Central Catholic in the 1930s, and had kept up a casual connection thereafter. Moreover, Danny and Georgie were the only other boys I knew from North Point Breeze who went to school with me at Holy Rosary and whose parents could afford to send them to summer camp. It was the planning, preparation, and finally the experience of being away from home together at camp a couple of summers that helped to cement our friendship, until their family moved out of the city to Churchill. The two brothers lived in an enormous house together with their parents and older sister, Mary Rita. That house is still there, but it has become for me a monument to the changing expectations of us all.

We boys spent untold hours exploring every part of that sizable property, and when we found a spot we liked, we stayed in or on it with ever a new game detailed to the occasion. There was the big back yard with its huge mulberry tree we climbed in, it seemed every day. In season we devoured its berries until we could hold no more and were frequently surprised on our trips to the bathroom, sometimes even before. The cement driveway was two lanes wide and traversed the length of the property, a veritable rollerskaters' paradise, all the way back from the boulevard to the three-car garage built into the hillside at the back of the estate. The house itself was flanked by a great side porch with its ceramic tile floor, enclosed by glass and varnished wood, surrounded by magnificent rhododendrons and spreading yews. That porch was stately to look at but seldom used, and that was a good thing for us boys.

We ten-year-olds preferred much more the underside of that veranda, where, in the low space under its deck, we had our secret cave. It was always dark down there and we had to use flashlights to creep around, but we whiled away many an inclement day there, sometimes discovering the decomposing remains of some critter who had had the misfortune of running into the dog, or some poison, or just some bad luck. Most importantly of all, we thought that nobody knew where we were or what we were up to. Of course, we never suspected that anyone on or even near could hear every word we said through the simple wooden lattice that served us as an impenetrable wall for us. Hmm, I wonder if Mary Rita overheard any secrets that she might want to share with me after all these years.

The whole McGannon house, all three floors of it, radiated out from the central great hall, which was open, as I recall it, to the very top of the house. It was in this vast expanse that, at the beginning of December each year, they put up the biggest Christmas tree I have ever seen in anyone's home, the Whitehouse included! I don't know how they ever trimmed it, much less how they got it inside, but I'm sure their maid and several workers from Mr. McGannon's foundry must have spent most of a day hanging off high ladders with no little daring. I could never count the myriad ornaments it required; its popcorn streamers alone could have satisfied a movie theatre!

The greatest place in the whole house was the third floor where the boys each had a bedroom. When I was allowed to stay overnight with Danny, it was in his room that we could watch late night TV until the test pattern woke us up. Just imagine: a ten-year-old with his own TV set in his bedroom! (Back then, I mean!) One excellent time we watched a movie with Red Skelton and Martha Raye as a young couple. We couldn't believe how old that film must have been, since every week we watched a much heavier and grayer Red Skelton do his sea gull and old bum routines, and knew Ms. Raye more as a large-mawed comedienne than a comely and eligible young heroine.

Downstairs, our favorite room was the den, a large and dark space with a heavy paneling of oak. It had those bookcases with glass windows that slide out and pull down in front, although I don't remember a whole lot of reading going on at that residence. Here we watched television a good deal on rainy days, or paged through Life or Look Magazine if it was early afternoon and all those boring soap operas were on. We occasionally wandered into the kitchen to hunt for food, without the help of Mrs. McGannon, who always left us to ourselves.

I don't ever remember seeing a cook there, but then, according to RULE NO. 3, I was always home for supper. The kitchen was backed by a porch on which an outside wooden staircase led up to the second floor. Perhaps that's where the maid lived and kept herself in hiding whenever the two terrors and I came snooping around the scene of her cookery.

Anyway, the kitchen is where I saw something that really struck me. One day, late in the afternoon, Mr. McGannon walked in on us there. He politely said hello, opened the fridge and grabbed a beer. When he opened it, he threw the cap half-way across the room into a basket for a perfect two points. He next reached up to a cupboard overhead at the sink, brought out a bottle—bourbon, I think—and a shot glass. He poured himself one, knocked it off, poured another, and proceeded with it and the beer into his office off the den. Now our family was no temperance league, to be sure, but the matter-of-factness of it all struck me. The routineness and casual attitude of George McGannon consuming that much booze by himself and without ceremony reminds one of how in the 1950s hard drinking was the order of the day. Having a drink or two before supper each day was considered quite natural, at least in the Irish families we knew, where hospitality meant a warm handshake at the door, a take your hat, and "What'll you have?"

The McGannons were the first of many, many good families to move away as the old neighborhood began to change. They built a terrific sprawling ranch-type place out in Churchill which I visited once or twice, but then we, too, moved out of the City. Mr. McGannon must have had quite a bit of trouble unloading that big old house in such an unsure neighborhood, but after a while the place went to a religious group of Italian priests called the Consolata Fathers. The Fathers wanted to have enough space to house the many vocations they expected to reap in the Pittsburgh area, where at that time so many good Catholic families were sending one or more of their numerous children to either minor seminary or a religious convent. Of course, the Fathers never attained their dream, for the vocation boom began to fizzle out just as they got organized to foster vocations in the late 1960's.

There's an urban legend that neither we kids nor even Mr. and Mrs. McGannon ever heard about. I heard somewhere that all that time there was a brick tunnel that ran from its blocked up entrance in their cellar up to a house behind it on Meade Street, allegedly once the home of the daughter of the original owner who expected his family to remain there for generations! How many secrets and surprises life holds! The old McGannon house is a monument to the unfulfilled expectations of us all. It stands largely empty of its builder's hopes, of the joy and laughter of the McGannons and their many, many friends, the friendly jokes of the cops that often stopped in the late afternoon for a drink, and of the hopes of the Consolata Fathers in America whose enterprise never really took off (no sci-fi allusion intended!). Really, the Sixties changed just about everything, didn't they?

4 – Grace's Chevy

The kind of trouble Nicky and I got into was mostly innocent, like the time were making our usual rounds of the neighborhood on a hot summer day, looking for something to do. We came upon Grace's 1949 Chevy, parked as it always was, in the alley behind the Sheedy's big house. Rather than the newer styling, Grace had chosen the old-fashioned Fleetline type with what we might today call a fastback, namely, the back end was formed in one continuous sweep from the roof to the rear bumper. Such a large blank surface formed by that big blue trunk was just begging to be put to use by us two eight-year-olds. So we each picked up a piece of mud and had a fun game of tic-tac-toe right above the fancy script of "Chevrolet" above the old-style handle you turned to open the trunk. The game ended in a tie—it took a few more years to figure out why it always did—and we moved on up the alley.

A day later Dad mentioned to me that the neighbors' maid had had her car scratched up on the trunk and that Nicky and I had been seen in the vicinity about the time when it must have happened. I said I didn't know anything about it, but went secretly down the alley at the first opportunity to have a look at it myself. One player's marks had been eliminated, evidently by a good washing. It was, after all, only mud. Part of the grid, however, and all of the X's were permanently etched in the blue paint. Evidently one of the chunks of mud was composed of more than just mud. And guess which player was X's?

I was able to continue my secret through one more interrogation in which Dad was really pressing for a confession, he telling me of the terrible consequences of lying to your parents. He had chosen the moment of confrontation while he was giving me a haircut, using the informality of the situation and my necessary fixity to the haircut stool to his best advantage—I could only give away my guilt by squirming. There was no getting away from the grilling by making up some excuse. Well, getting a haircut from Dad was an uncomfortable experience at any time, so my physical and emotional discomfort made it easy to burst into tears and end the tension by sniveling, "Would I lie to you?"

That seems to have checked Dad's suspicions, and I thought I was in the clear—that is, until Nicky cracked under I don't know what pressure from his dad. (Come to think of it, Mr. Criss was a lawyer!) Unbeknownst to me, he had spilled all the beans and his dad had evidently informed mine.

Now for a long time I wondered why I told such a boldfaced lie. I've thought about this a lot, and have noted that some of the greatest liars were Catholic. I think it has something to do with our long-running moral teaching of "double effect." This principle allows a just person to perform an action which has both good and bad effects, as long as the intended part of the act is for the good, while the evil effect is what we might today call "collateral damage." This is a good and logical principle of decision making, since it takes into account the complexity of actions in the real world, but it is patently a grand target for abuse.

Now I know that at eight years old I didn't have a very well formed and philosophical moral theory, but I'm sure that many a lie has been told by a Catholic boy (and others, too!) like me, based on this very Catholic ethical principle, whether we were aware of it or not.

You see, I knew that I had not, not even in the slightest way, intended to scratch Grace's car. I was a good boy, and I never would do such a thing! But I thought that if I admitted that I had been responsible for the damage to the trunk, it would appear that I was a bad, more than mischievous kid, deserving of strong punishment—of which I was clearly not! The lie was just the part of the action not directly intended when compared to the good effect of sparing me from a very harsh and unjust punishment. 'N'at. (This means *et cetera* in Western PA).

Parents ought to give a child some options, and must clearly explain the consequences of each. Give the kid a way out of the mess or he/she will lie, since a kid can only interpret this kind of situation as "Mom or Dad is really mad at me for this." We can all agree that it is a very bad thing to have lied to a parent. Use a good old Catholic distinction between penance and reparation: a merely negative punishment (penance) is minimally effective for future behavior, but when honesty is lauded, some kind of reparation can be worked out that might serve equally well as the punishment expected, but have a positive effect on character instead. What eventually happened in this case was that I was told never to lie again and had to give up my allowance to pay for the new paint job. That terrible condition lasted only a few weeks, and the whole matter was soon forgotten. It was an episode that no one was proud of. It was easily dispensed with down the chute of oblivion.

5 – The Great Buckeye War

Our street had the best buckeye trees in Pittsburgh. They were surely the biggest around, probably planted back in 1905 as part of the Westinghouse Park Plan when the six great homes were constructed. No street I knew had a bigger number of them. They lined our whole block with lush dark green foliage, and I can still see the myriads of florets on the tall white candles they pushed out when they blossomed every Spring. They gave the Boulevard a luxurious and verdant canopy that kept us cool all summer, but every autumn they produced a sea of detritus of oversized brown fronds that the street cleaners piled into waist high mounds for a fleet of trucks to take them away.

We never really thought about the buckeyes as these large seeds ripened all summer long in the big trees, but when the first husk split and a shiny chestnut appeared on the ground, every boy in the neighborhood jumped into action. Then we gladly dedicated our last days of freedom before school started to an all-out harvest of the shiny brown treasure. Little did we know that later that summer our yearly harvest would bring about an occasion of true evil in our young lives.

Our method of collection was rather direct: before the buckeyes could open of themselves and drop to the ground (where some other boys might grab them up!) we gathered all kinds of missiles to fling at the stately trees to knock our treasure down. Bricks, footballs, and various sticks were used, but my personal favorite was a foot-long piece of two-by-four from Dad's workshop. It was just heavy enough and just big enough for a ten-year-old to control in flight and still give a big wallop when it hit. You had to be sure there was no car passing by because when you launched the missiles from the high terrace of the front yard; the full force we used to get the whole cluster at a single shot could carry through the limbs and well onto the boulevard. Now Thomas was a very wide street and had only a trickle of traffic, but especially if you missed buckeye and branch, your projectile could, and sometimes did, scare the daylights out of a passing motorist.

My best friend Nicky Criss and I were together every day, but at buckeye time the inseparable duo swelled to include Nicky's little brother Russ and Denny Sheedy from two houses away. These guys were younger, and didn't dare because of us older boys, to gather buckeyes on their own, but they were happy to work with us in this noble endeavor for a couple of summers. The best trees were in front of our house, seven of them, still bearing fruit when last I looked, although the house is long gone, a casualty of the changing nature of south Homewood, or "North Point Breeze" as people now call it for snobbish reasons.

There was one brownish tree with very small buckeyes at the end of our row and I remember being very angry at the poor thing because of its ugly russet color and diminutive yield. It was, as a matter fact, the only real Ohio buckeye of the lot. All the others were the more magnificent horse chestnut, splendid in the verdure of their foliage and its clusters of florets, proffering an extra large yield of the nuts, sometimes even a prized triple-header. Well, they were all buckeye trees to us and that was just one that couldn't measure up. We took its fruit, don't worry, always being thorough in our childish efficiency.

One year we managed to collect enough buckeyes to completely fill a great white packing crate Nicky's family stored in their garage, what with exclusive rights to our trees and what we could grab from the many trees over in the park. That seems to have been the beginning of our downfall. Some older boys from up the street either saw us lugging bags full of the lucre home from the park or heard about it from the insidious girls in our families, but at any rate they challenged our bragging rights to the biggest cache of the year. When we reluctantly showed them the truth, that our vast hoard simply humiliated their paltry collection, we had trouble on our hands. Before we knew it they decided to use some of their now worthless buckeyes to fling at us, taking potshots at odd times when we would pass up or down the alley on our way to McCarthy's Drug Store or to play with other friends on Murtland Ave. or Meade St.

The leader of this gang of four or five was a boy named Timmy, and he was older and bigger than us. When once he hit one of us with a buckeye it really hurt, we would not back down without a fight. In our innocence of such things as fighting, we decided to take them on in an all-out battle—like you saw on TV. After all, we had far more ammunition and could surely outlast them.

We loaded up our paperboy sacks with plenty of ammunition and stalked up the alley to meet the enemy. We came upon them skulking behind their garage hangout and charged with much yelling and bravado. They didn't back away, but sent a hail of stinging missiles our way in return, their own arsenal at the ready. A well-aimed shot whapped me pretty hard on the arm. Blinded with rage, I groped for the largest buckeye in my sack. I flung it with all my force at Timmy, my opposite number in this combat. When I saw how wide the reactionary missile was of the mark, I instantly calmed down with the knowledge that rage is no ally to the effective infliction of injury.

In my mind I stopped the action around me, selected a handy-sized projectile, aimed and threw with good but moderate force, and Timmy yelped in pain. One buckeye after the other left my hand with the cold accuracy of a target shooter in a gallery of moving objects. I got a couple of solid hits in, but the battle didn't last very long. Somebody (I forget who, but it must have been one of our group) got hurt, hit in the face. We went running home, taking the problem to the highest arbitration, Dad. Dad became very upset and scolded us forcefully, not so much for doing something wrong to other people but for doing something so dangerous to ourselves. He sent everyone packing with the warning that their parents would hear about this.

That very night he went up-street right into Timmy's house to clarify the situation with whoever was in charge of that household. Whatever he said to Timmy's parents must have worked, for we hardly ever even saw those boys again. In all honesty, I think they must have shifted their stomping grounds to one of the other boys' houses. It was as if they all had moved to a different part of town.

We were all very relieved. I for one had really scared myself when that real hate raised its repulsive head within me. I saw for the first time the ugly fact that I really wanted to hurt that boy, and intuited the danger and unremitting ferocity that could ensue if someone else felt the same way and gave in to the anger. It was a detestable experience I wish I had never been a part of, and totally uncharacteristic of our kind of hijinks in the small world on the two sides of Lark Way. Maybe we were just growing up, but the next year there was no enthusiasm at all for buckeyes.

Part 3 – Church

1 – Holy Rosary

Our next big topic is "church." I have deliberately chosen the word we used back then to include all things religious, and there was quite a bit of that in our lives at 6928. We used the word "church" because "religion" or "the Christian faith" would have sounded too Protestant to us in those days. We weren't "Christians"; we were "Catholics" for God' sake!

"Church" was a way of life for us, our local incarnation of all things associated with being a Catholic in the 1950s: mass, religious devotions, priests, nuns, parochial school, altar boys, choir boys, morality, sacraments, clubs and sodalities, and—how could I forget it?—fundraising. Last of all, "church" meant that there was a large international organization headed by the Pope (Pius XII at the time) and operated by all the clergy, but populated by all the lay Catholics in their parishes.

Now from a theological point of view, this is really an interesting use of the word "church." While an awful lot of people in the Fifties thought "the Church" meant the Vatican, the hierarchy, and other Catholic officialdom, we sort of foreshadowed the Second Vatican Council at Holy Rosary in retaining a more primitive idea of church. The Council, which lay still years in the future, made popular the New Testament idea of church as *ekklesia*, or assembly of the people called out by God. The Council Fathers thus restored at least the concept of it to the official language of Catholics, if not to our lives. Our 1950s use of the term was less personal than that, but we knew in our hearts that the church was us, and especially what we did in our days in our "Church."

The physical plant of Holy Rosary was truly splendid. It still is, although the name was changed to St. Charles Lwanga to be more suitable to the later members of the worshipping community in Homewood. Sadly, the church has been closed now by the Catholic Diocese of Pittsburgh for lack of membership and support. There, filling almost an entire block of Kelly Street, stands the big grammar school, the magistral rectory and the absolutely splendid church edifice, with the convent across the alley, its front on Hamilton Avenue, next to the local branch of the Carnegie library.

Our "church" was dedicated to Our Lady of the Most Holy Rosary, but everybody called it simply "Holy Rosary." First and foremost was the church itself, a marvelous edifice that imposed itself grandly in that neighborhood of small working-class homes. The church and its mansion of a rectory were a tribute to all the longing for acceptance into the middle class by the blue-collar men and women who built the church just as the Great Depression hit.

The edifice was completed in 1930, the product of famous Boston architect Ralph Adams Cram and the donations of all those hard-working parishioners at the beginning of the last century. It is a marvel of neo-Gothic fantasy of Spanish inspiration, large in both its conception and execution, unique in design and rich in every detail of its ornamentation, its slender pillars, its patterned marble floors, its oaken pews and the heavy wainscoting of the sanctuary, its organ magnificent both in appearance and sonance. It was said to be "a restatement of the Cathedral of Burgos in Spain" with one great spire, a striking array of pinnacles and a superb corner porch, a wonder for such a modest congregation, Irish and German mainly, who evidently thought that nothing was too good for God when they started the church in the 1920s.

Beside it, connected by a special covered passageway, the rectory is a beautiful house, a mansion really, spacious and majestic with a fine, large yard. It was executed before the church, about the same time and with the same turn-of-the-century rich decor as our home on Thomas Blvd. It was loaded with heavy oak and mahogany woodwork, yet very airy with its multitude of windows. The rectory's first floor had several offices and parlors, a formal dining room, but no real living room. Of course, it had a large kitchen, with the cook's quarters in the back. The priests never entertained in the rectory, but each had a private suite including a sitting room for their armchair, desk and television.

A great part of the second floor was dedicated to the regal chambers of the pastor, including a grand sitting room that stretched, as I recall it, all the way across the front of the house. Few mortal men (and surely no women) were ever admitted into that sacrosanct precinct, but as the pastor's pet altar boy and a seminarian-to-be, I saw its parlor once, when Monsignor sent me to fetch a picture book from his desk up there. I dawdled just long enough to see the first color television set I'd only heard about, the biggest and best that RCA made!

I remember the dining room mostly, for I was often invited for breakfast by Monsignor. I was frequently at the rectory's formal breakfast table on Saturdays after Mass before my Latin lesson and truly enjoyed being served on the fine china and crystal. There was always lots of orange juice and oatmeal, then the bacon and eggs made by Anne the housekeeper just the way I liked them.

Monsignor would ring a little crystal bell whenever he wanted Anne to come in and clear when we were finished with a course or when he wanted more coffee. I think he treated me better than the associate priests—I never saw them at breakfast those Saturday mornings. Fr. Spelman once laughingly said that in that house I ranked above the assistants, which meant somewhere between Anne the housekeeper and Vicar (pronounced in Latin VEE-kahr), Monsignor's big Doberman.

Back in the alley the separate double garage was quite large, but only ever had room for Monsignor's huge Chrysler Imperial (never more than two model years old!) and an array of first-rate lawn and snow maintenance equipment. The convent across the alley is huge, and it had to be, since it housed over two dozen Sisters of St. Joseph in its heyday. I don't know what it is used for today.

Together, the two residences made up quite a religious population center just west of the little business district of Homewood, but much more than that, they gave a rich presence, a leadership, and an enormous sense that things were as they should be, for the parish's several thousand Catholic adults and children. The parish was for many years the largest in the Pittsburgh Diocese. This was the ultimate immigrant success story, with a culture of excellence of life along with deep religious piety that made us so proud to be Holy Rosary Church. All this succeeded in creating an impressive Catholic cultural center in Homewood. A considerable number of priests, religious, doctors, lawyers, teachers and other professionals got their start at Holy Rosary through its highpoint in the 1950s and beyond. One of its greatest assets was the Holy Rosary Grammar School which deserves its own full description in Part 4 of our book.

2 – Monsignor

At the center, and indisputably in charge of the whole world of "church" activity, of the spiritual (and sometimes material) welfare of the Catholic population of Homewood, was the Right Reverend Monsignor Henry A. Carlin, P. A., or simply and unmistakenly "Monsignor." It was never "the Monsignor" or Monsignor Carlin"—just "Monsignor," and everybody in the 13th ward of Pittsburgh knew who you were talking about. The appellation was invariable pronounced "Mont-SEEN-yer," and without exaggeration, invariably struck fear into the hearts of those upon whomever its unquestionable authority was thrust. Whenever an argument occurred, it could be terminated quite definitively by the two words: "Monsignor said!"

Although he grew up on a farm in Sutersville in Westmoreland County, Monsignor was a gentleman, and by his priesthood a member of the Irish nobility. His demeanor was always most proper and his carriage bespoke his unquestioned importance. He was more English than Irish in the way he acted, but he was the epitome of what every Irishman wanted in a supreme leader. What I mean is this: he didn't have any trace of a brogue, he didn't meddle in politics—at least not in any public forum, and there was nothing like a private circle of friends. He simply carried himself with extreme self-confidence and expected to be catered to and obeyed in every occasion. He never wheedled or harangued his congregation, but whenever he addressed his flock from the high pulpit at Holy Rosary Church, he simply stated his mind with the unflappable assurance of personal infallibility.

Actually, he didn't preach much. He often left that to the assistant priests, all of whom were aware that he was listening to every word, checking for orthodoxy. He would do this whether he was himself presiding at the altar, or, with the help of a speaker system in the rectory, listening from the grand dining room as he dined regally, attended by his devoted housekeeper, Anne. He was quite clear in his leadership of his assistant priests and ran the Rectory as a tight ship.

Besides holy Mass, there was one devotion that was very dear to Monsignor. During Lent he would preach the Stations of the Cross every Friday night. Notice, I didn't say "lead" the Stations, or "make" them. He definitely preached them. Monsignor would enter the sanctuary with a contingent of altar boys and go directly to the pulpit where he presided, while the servers with cross and candles would go round the church and stop at each of the fourteen "stations" of the prayer.

The stations themselves were imaged in rather well-done bas reliefs, each with an embedded wooden cross—attractive and very clear in content. Monsignor would lead the usual prayers for each one like any other priest, but in addition to that he would preach a meditation on each one of these moments of the Passion of Christ: "Consider how Jesus was pierced with sorrow as he left the Holy City bearing the heavy cross for our sins!" The whole exercise could easily take an hour.

Monsignor was perhaps the only good example of the old-style preaching I've ever heard. He was eloquent; he was moving; and he was loud! I can remember the cadences of his voice as he whispered an intimate detail that you could hardly hear and then roared out how Jesus suffered for us at each point along the way of the cross. In those days, too, you could hear a pin drop during his sermon in the always packed eleven o'clock Mass on Sundays. He always wrapped a silver rosary around his left hand, giving an additional flash of light to his gesticulations, often pounding the ambo where his written text lay unopened.

Sometimes, overcome with tears, he would have to stop while all of us held our breath until the master speaker could continue his line of thought. He told of post-World War II refugees offering him something to eat if only the priest from the great liberating country of America would come into their dirt-floored hovel to share a moment of prayer and impart a blessing on their house.

His was a deep faith! He communicated to us expertly and effectively, demonstrating with his voice the kind of suffering Jesus must have known and undergone out of love for us. Two rusty old railroad spikes often appeared in his gnarled fist as he expostulated on the horror of the crucifixion. "So great was the pain of sacrifice in his divinity that no mere human could have undergone it," he would say. The Stations were a very moving service for all of us, young and old alike, nor did we ever miss the Wednesday night Novenas at Holy Rosary.

At all times and in every location of Holy Rosary Monsignor always wore his prelatial black cassock with its thirty-three crimson red buttons down the front, crossed by the huge magenta sash, its satin watermark gamboling in the light as he moved. When on rare occasion he did appear in a plain black clerical suit, it was well-tailored and with a full clerical vest topped by a #19 pontiff Roman collar. The French cuffs extended just so from the sleeve of the jacket to flash large and jeweled cufflinks. Then he would fire up his presidential Chrysler Imperial kept alone in the rectory's spacious garage, with nary a word as to where or why he was going, least of all to the assistant priests left in charge. Of course, they had been duly informed of what they had and what they had not the authority to do in his absence.

It was great when he took the altar boys, or rather a select few of us, to his family's farm, where his two maiden sisters still lived. They were always very nice to us, and offered sweet, chilled lemonade and great, fresh oatmeal and raisin cookies for us to feast upon. His sisters gave us the run of the place, including an old barn, long bereft of any animals, but still filled with hay for us to jump and play in. Rather permissive of Monsignor, you might say, to stay on the front porch with his kin and chat while we boys were off on our own? Possibly irresponsible, with us cavorting in that old barn, you say? Then you never knew Monsignor! Rough-housing, dangerous antics, a boyish tussle that could turn into a shoving match that could get someone hurt? They were as unthinkable as suicide!

How would you explain to your parents if Monsignor read them down for your behavior? After they got out of the psych ward in the hospital and recovered from the shock treatments they would need to recover, you knew you'd be flogged to within an inch of your life and grounded until you were thirty-five!

The P.A. after Monsignor's name stood for Prothonotary Apostolic, "the highest honor a priest could receive short of being named a bishop," we were told. He was never raised to the latter ecclesiastical niveau, but for many years he was Vicar General of the Diocese of Pittsburgh. And well did he take to the new high honor. With the P. A. title came all the regalia of a bishop, without the canonical status, of course, but what did Monsignor need with more power? All he really needed were the insignia. And display them he did! On all possible liturgical occasions (high feast days) he would preside at a solemn high Mass in the full glory this office conveyed.

He really made quite an appearance! To fully describe him I have to start at the bottom: he would be shod in velvet buskins, special high-topped slippers in all colors of the liturgical year: green for ordinary time, white for glorious feasts, purple for Lent, and red for celebrations of the Holy Spirit. The elegant pair of matching velvet gloves, worn in procession to and from the altar, necessitated a double set of rings, one for everyday wear and one to fit over the glove, since the regular ring would be too narrow. Of miters he had several, and I honestly remember different colors, although those who study those bygone days assure me that such could not have been the case.

The man knew how to use power effectively and had his own special sense of irony. When a prominent lawyer who lived in our neighborhood died unexpectedly in 1957, there was a huge funeral at St. Bede's Church. Now it was common practice for Catholics who lived in our neighborhood to worship at St. Bede's, often going even as far as Sacred Heart in Shadyside, because they considered themselves more at home with the gentry of those parishes than with the working class membership of Holy Rosary. (They also gave their weekly offering envelope to said churches as well!) The canonical lines of Holy Rosary Parish, however, ran all the up to Penn Avenue, including said lawyer's residence.

Friends and neighbors had provided all manner of food for the family and mourners, and since the funeral happened to occur on a Friday, a dispensation to eat meat would be required from the pastor. This was no unusual request and was normally readily granted, so the widow dutifully called Fr. Enwright at St. Bede's Rectory. He said, however, that she would need to get permission from Monsignor Carlin, since he was her legal pastor. When she called Holy Rosary rectory Monsignor answered the phone. When she made her entreaty known to him he replied, "You are correct Mrs. Reilly, yes, I am indeed your pastor, and the answer to your request is No"! That was it! There was no arguing with Monsignor.

The great man, however, did have a kind side, too. There were several families who were able to tough out hard times because of the parish's well-known charity. Then, too, Monsignor would deign to make an appearance over at the school in his grand black cassock with the red piping and buttons, always girded round by its great satin sash. Once in a while, I'm sure, he might even have heard what a child was saying.

At the beginning of my seventh grade, when I started talking about going to the Minor Seminary, Monsignor insisted that I get a jump on things by learning Latin, with himself as my tutor. He said we should meet on Saturday mornings after the 8:00 Mass, and that I would be invited to breakfast at the rectory. Of course, he didn't ask if I wanted to learn Latin, nor did he consult my parents. I simply conveyed Monsignor's request to my folks and started coming to church every Saturday morning.

Now I have studied many languages over the years and have had lessons in most of them, but I have never had a worse teacher than dear Monsignor. How can I forget that first lesson? There was no textbook or introduction of any kind. Monsignor just printed out for me the first declension and pronounced it, "*Femina, feminae, feminae, feminam, femina,*" and told me to memorize these forms—without the slightest hint to this twelve-year-old as to what in the blazes they were forms of! He would then show off by making me parrot them to unsuspecting parishioners who would nod and coo in wonder at what incredible things Monsignor could bring about.

The next lesson was the first verbal conjugation (whatever that was supposed to be!) "*Laudo, laudas, laudat*," I played back with my child's awesome power of pure rote memory, but here I somehow managed to grasp the significance of the inflections, surely because of Sr. Judith's classes in grammar. I got it from her explanation of the English subjunctive with its odd form "he go." Oh yes, we actually learned grammar at Holy Rosary Grammar School, diagramming sentences, too! At any rate, the whole process came together a bit for me and made freshman Latin quite a breeze the next year at the "Little Seminary" in Buffalo.

All in all, Monsignor was an unforgettable personage, an icon in our Catholic understanding of dignity and authority. I don't know of anybody like him anymore. He was, in fact, born too late even in his own time. Several priests have told me that with his great intelligence and talent he would have been made a bishop in an earlier era, but that he was just too strict and by-the-book for the already changing times in the decade before the Second Vatican Council. He used to brag that he hadn't read a book since his seminary days where he excelled at study and had committed to memory all that he needed to know.

We loved him, in an awed kind of way, and were very proud that he was our pastor. He taught us well the goodness of rectitude and the assurance of always doing the right thing in his bigger-than-life presence. In his own way he manifested to us the powerful love and paternal surety of God. I hope you are smiling with me now, Monsignor, and I offer you the thanks a child can never give to those who so love and nurture them.

3 – Altar Boys

Being selected to be an altar boy at Holy Rosary was a great privilege reserved only for the "good" boys who attended parochial school. There were, of course, no girl altar servers back then. Not even thought of! Boys who went to the public school (we actually called it "Protestant School!") obviously could not be trusted to be reverent enough for the altar. After all, if they were religious, and therefore knew how to be reverent, why weren't they going to Catholic school? It was free to all parishioners! Their parents obviously did not take the interest in their children that punctual arrival at altar boy practices and the services would require.

Even though the new boys were sometimes trained by one of the more minor nuns, everyone knew that behind the selection of every new server was the Sister-in-charge of all the altar boys, Sr. Judith. She had absolute authority—under Monsignor of course—in the administration of the whole enterprise of service at the altar at Holy Rosary. Sr. Judith was very serious about what it meant to serve at the altar, but she had a real kindness in her, and later I will talk about what a fine teacher she was. We knew we could trust Sr. Judith to be reasonable and correct in her judgment, but God help you if you were ever the reason for something going wrong on the altar!

Every detail of the serving duty was spelled out for us, from what we wore to the Latin we parroted, to exactly what we were supposed to do and when, and exactly how it was to be done. Nothing was left to personal preference. There was only one right way to kneel down when serving at the altar: one started by bending the right (never the left) knee and touching it to the floor as the left leg bent to be folded down to the floor as well, but only after balance was maintained by contact with the floor by the right knee. Getting up was accomplished equally without any wobbling by the reverse procedure: left knee raised and left foot planted firmly on the floor exactly beside the right knee which then came up directly along the left leg until the foot could be placed flat on the floor, again without any wobble.

There was a dress code, of course. All the boys were to present themselves for vesting in black (newly shined!) dress shoes, with black socks, black pants with your shirt collar turned under ("No collars sticking out, please!"). Most of us had special "server shoes" which were kept with a perfect shine because they were never worn for anything except when serving. As for the pants, they were always cleaned and pressed, and there really wasn't much call for a kid to wear black pants outside of serving, anyway.

Why not just come to church in a clean tee shirt? Are you kidding?! Wearing just a jersey to church was about as unthinkable as serving in tennis shoes, even though our high-tops back then were always black. When we moved to Buffalo in 1959 the pastor there had all the altar boys wear white sneakers to serve. I could only nod my head at the laxity of that undignified, suburban church. Although I was only thirteen, and already in the Minor Seminary, it never occurred to be a part of such a minor league altar boy program.

Vesting for serving Mass at Holy Rosary was always the same: you chose a black cassock from the rack in the boys' sacristy and carefully checked in the low mirror, placed there for just that purpose, that the hem arrived exactly at your ankles (not above, not below). You were assigned a simple white surplus for your Mom to wash, starch and iron once a week for daily mass, but each and every time for a Sunday or holy day service.

The get-up for solemn mass occasions was exceptional. In fact, the whole ceremony was designed to be a magnificent imitation of the heavenly liturgy of the Church Triumphant in heaven itself! For the pontifical solemn mass, the large sanctuary overflowed. In addition to Monsignor, presiding in all his colorful regalia that I have already described, there would be two other priests fulfilling the roles of deacon and subdeacon, each garbed in special vestments called dalmatics, fashioned from the same exquisite material as Monsignor's chasuble and showing the different rank of each.

The lineup of altar boys was impressive: there were the cross bearer and his two acolytes bearing lit candles to lead of the procession headed by the thurifer, an older boy who carried the incense and thurible (or censer), the contrivance that held burning charcoal waiting for the action of the presider to add the odiferous substance to be burned. Six torch bearers then led the way for at least thirty choir boys who would deploy to the choir stalls, most opulently fashioned in oaken pews for them in the extended sanctuary. Bringing up the rear, and immediately in front of the priests, came a mitre bearer, a ring bearer, and an older boy, the master of ceremonies who saw that all the other boys were doing what they were supposed to. If you're noticing that I haven't mentioned any girls at all, I won't. There were none.

All of these children were gussied up in a black cassock, a surplus, and a high Roman collar, starched to a solid state, worn externally and fitted with a large white silk bow. And they weren't just the ordinary surpluses either. On one of his trips to Europe Monsignor had brought, from Belgium I believe, a full set of gorgeous linen surpluses, with eight pleats across the front and eight pleats across the back, trimmed in red and with an embroidered gold cross encircled in red at the hem. We felt truly privileged to wear such a costume that probably cost as much as the entire dress-up wardrobes of many of the boys. This garment gave us a certain attitude on the altar, and I can't help but think of the Flornce Ziegfield story on the way he dressed his chorus line. When he ordered lace at the sleeves for the whole troupe, one of his accountants carped to him, "The audience can't tell that it's real lace!" Ziegfield replied, "Ah, but the girls can!"

Now, as for the Roman collar and the big, floppy bowtie, these were washed, starched and ironed by the Sisters, who also laundered the surpluses themselves, since no ordinary mother could be trusted with the care of such costly items of linen and silk. The silk bows were all pre-tied in a perfect shape, of course, and Sister snapped shut an elastic loop around the narrow clasp area on the collar in the front (that the priests usually turn around to the back to button up). To perfect the look Sister pinned down the bottom ends of the bows to your cassock under the corners of the collar to extend and show off the bow perfectly. And, oh yes, the collar itself had to be fastened with a real brass collar stud. I am sure that if Velcro had been invented back then, it would never have seen the inside of the sanctuary of Holy Rosary Church!

And who could forget how we learned the correct pronunciation and accent of the Latin prayers and responses that the altar boys had to memorize for daily mass. Remember: the congregation was completely passive in those days. The main action was taking place in the sanctuary, separated from the nave of the church by a railing. It was the juvenile altar boys who made the correct responses for the adults! "*Et coom SPEE-ree-too TOO-oh.*" I remember the transliterations in the little red altar boy book very well: that the Latin *Quia tu es Deus* appeared as "*KWEE-ah too ez DAY-oos*" made no difference to us at all—we didn't know what we were saying, anyway. What we did know was that performance counted. It was not a matter of comprehension. Besides, like the congregation we had no interest in understanding the Latin. The words were the same every time, so you didn't have to translate them when you attended (not "celebrated" as we say today) Mass. You just had to have a good idea of what usually went on at a certain part of the Mass, as the words were as much a part of the mystery as the inscrutable circles and crosses the priest made in the air facing the wall with his back to his people!

The whole solemn Mass thing was pretty impressive, however, and the practices for it were often even longer than the event itself! The classic illustration of the whole process for me was the protocol of the thurifer (censer bearer) at such a celebration. First of all, you knew that it was a great privilege to handle the incense and thurible (the censer itself), and only a few of the older boys ever attained to it. The regulations for the thurifer included all the basics required of all the boys: whether standing in place or on the move, your carriage had to be straight at all times; scratching and twisting about were to be kept to the absolute minimum. When you genuflected you never shifted your weight so that your shoulder slumped; you accomplished the entire "reverence" without the slightest inclination of the upper torso. We had to practice that obeisance over and over, both at altar boy practice and at home till we got it right. I doubt if the average middle-aged person could perform it correctly!

Bows, I mean the inclination of head and shoulders, were either "profound" or simplex, depending on what was reverenced by them, but they were to be solemnly performed whatever the case! The profound bow, used only in saying the Confiteor and at the *Et incarnatus est* in the Creed, meant bending from the waist. The more usual simplex bow was a slight but respectful inclination of the shoulders and head. You had to know when to do all the "bows" of the Gloria and Credo by heart. That meant that just before certain phrases in the Latin came up you had to be ready to bow and then to un-bow, to straighten back up, at just the right moment when the text was completed.

For the rest, you just had to remember to bow simply before and after every action you did for the priest. Of course, hands were always "folded" in front of the chest (your "breast" as the Sisters called it). This meant that one's open hands were pressed together with the fingers perfectly straight and the thumbs crossed (right over left and never left over right!). The only crooked fingers ever tolerated were those of Bernie Murphy whose fourth and fifth fingers had been broken as a child and healed wrongly. He got a special dispensation from Sister to have those two fingers, and only those two, less than perfectly straight.

Those were the basics. The thurifer, however, had the important task of opening and holding the censer while the priest laded in the incense. You always held your breath until you saw that the charcoal you had lit earlier was hot enough to produce a cloud of holy smoke. If you had started it too early it wouldn't last for the whole ceremony, but if you didn't get it started enough time before mass, it wouldn't burn hot enough—oh, what a calamity! The priest would have to smash it up and, God forbid, even blow on it, to get the thing smoking. There were regulations for the thurifer even when you weren't doing anything. Rest position was always on your knees at the southwest corner of the center black marble rectangle on the patterned sanctuary floor. From there you could give the host and the chalice each a set of three triple swings at their elevations at the Consecration.

You had to remember how to hold an "empty" censer (that is, with only the charcoal and no incense). Then you carried it by its ring with your left thumb. But after it was "filled" with incense and smoking away, you always used your right thumb. When you incensed the priest (or the people), you placed your right hand with the ring against your "breast" just on the left side. You grasped the chains at mid-length with your left hand just above the loop that gathered all three chains together and pressed it to your breast just below the ring so as to hold the whole thing up so that your right hand came free to grasp the chains just above the censer itself to then swing the bowl at the people.

When you grasped the chains you put your forefinger on top and the three others behind the chain. This way you could control the swing so that it made a slight clinking sound as you gave two swings at them, first two to the middle, then two to the left, then two to the right, not forgetting to finish off the gesture with a simplex bow as you had begun the act. No kidding! Could somebody make this up? How do I remember it all? How could I forget it!

When the ceremony was finally over, the thurifer moved deftly to the front of the pack after a barely perceptible nod from the emcee, in order to lead everyone in the "recession" out from the sanctuary, through the front aisle, and over to the sacristy.

Now in all of our rehearsals and other preparations for serving there was never a hint of what it was that we were doing with all of that rigamarole, much less how to participate spiritually in this most important sacrament of our religion. Herein, I think, lie the roots of so much formalism I have seen among many clerics. Here, too, is part of the reason so many Catholics long for the old Latin mass with all its mysteriousness. They, too, were never taught what was actually taking place at the ceremony. A pity they can't transcend the desire for awe in attending Mass for the more personal way of participating in it, in the joy at their redemption, giving thanks, as a more biblical eucharistic theology would have it. "Giving thanks" is what the Greek word *eucharistia* actually means, after all!

4 – The Great Fire

Early on a cold Friday morning in 1957 a friend called to tell us of a disaster in progress down at our church. The news spread among parishioners like its content. It was the Great Fire at Holy Rosary School! We turned on the radio for particulars, but we could already see the billows of black smoke five blocks away down over the railroad tracks at Holy Rosary. It didn't matter whether it was the church, rectory, convent or school—Holy Rosary was ablaze!

Within the hour the entire population of the parish who weren't already at work was down at the church growing in trepidation as the black smoke poured out of the school in increasing volume. The sisters organized the children, herding us all into the church, taking roll, and keeping a close lookout for anyone talking in the pews, a taboo for children and adults alike at Holy Rosary. The parents and other adults were thus free to go out and watch in readiness to do anything they could to help, knowing that us children were kept out of harm's way in the church a hundred yards away on the other side of the rectory. We sat in confused silence, then knelt when sister started the rosary, until finally there was a commotion in the back of the church.

Bill Burns, at that time Pittsburgh's leading news broadcaster, was there himself with a camera crew. In those days they used a film camera, but there was a sound hookup and Mr. Burns was doing a piece in the back of the church with muffled voice as the prayers continued. That night the coverage on television news was prolonged—everybody knew the importance of a fire at one of the City's great Catholic schools.

The city firemen attacked the fire with all their force and managed to contain it within the older part of the building, built originally as the church in 1900. Firetrucks from all over the East End of the City were positioned around the building, in the schoolyards, blocking both Kelly Street and the alley behind, with the sisters and the Salvation Army pouring coffee by the gallon and miraculously producing scores of meatless sandwiches—it was Friday, you know. The firemen brought the blaze under control by noon and within a few hours a massive cleanup was in progress. When all the "hotspots" had been picked at and doused, everyone who was able began coming down to school to help.

Fr. Lackner found himself in charge of a tremendous workforce and handled it brilliantly. He first took some of the men, went over to Murphy's Five and Ten Cent Store across the street and consigned every mop, broom, bucket and wringer in the store. Thus equipped the women started the incredible task of removing gallons of filthy water from the floors, stairs and landings of the basement, while the men, who had brought their own crowbars, sledgehammers and carpentry tools, started knocking down dangerous plaster, clearing the halls and boarding up windows and off-limits areas. They pulled debris out and away from the building and made tons of it disappear in a stream of trucks lent to the effort by a dozen local companies.

Fr. Lackner procured emergency lamps from somewhere and the various crews worked all night and all the next day, Saturday, cleaning and readying the building. School reopened on Monday morning after a miracle of organized and generous assistance by every able-bodied man and woman of the parish, who worked in four and six-hour shifts to make the place presentable, no, more than that, to make it ready for school as usual. Since most of the real damage had been to the basement and the old gym, it was just a matter of hard work to clean up and air out the classrooms. I don't know if school was abbreviated that Monday, but I do know that we never had to make up for a single day lost.

Fr. Lackner related to me, as we were chatting about the Great Fire at a later time, that the owner of one of the big cleaning companies who lived in the parish said to him, "Father, you can have a job as foreman in my company anytime you want," so quickly and thoroughly had he led the cleanup. The real miracle, however, was the sense of unity, the cooperation, and the devotion of the people of Holy Rosary. The same spirit held true in the drive to rebuild (and improve) the facility to its maximum serviceability. The whole parish got involved in that endeavor with our Dad at the helm. That's how I know that all the money was raised and the school completely renovated by the next September start of schoolyear.

One hardly ever sees that kind of unity. I can say in all honesty that people never questioned their duty to be there and to do and to give all they could to refurbish their school and guarantee its continuance as a central part of our Catholic community. That kind of identification is hard to find now, perhaps because the word "parochial" really had a good meaning back then. The stability the old parish gave was extraordinary, even as it sometimes precluded wider horizons of thought and activity. In the sweeping changes that started to occur with the amalgamation of parishes in the 1980s so much disappeared of that Catholic identity, for our own good sometimes, but too often for our loss.

5 – Home Mass

Long before the Second Vatican Council demystified the eucharistic liturgy, making it more accessible to the faithful both in its language and the possibility of an occasional intimate setting, we Maloney kids were celebrating "home" masses, that is, the holy sacrifice of the Mass in the informal locale of the home. And we performed them with all the enthusiasm that liturgists today would call a most meaningful and appropriate expression of the sacred action. This prescience of the liturgical renewal came instinctively from our great love of the Mass and an intuition of the fittingness of its celebration, on special occasions, in the sacred center of our home.

The Catholic Fathers of Vatican Council II were able to appreciate the liturgy once again as a sacramental memorial of the Last Supper of Jesus, and bring its communal significance as sacred banquet to the forefront. Now we kids hadn't the faintest notion of that advanced theology, but performed our childish take on the rite with all the reverence and formality of a high church service, imitating the sacrosanct ritual of the priests and their designated acolytes we knew so well. Interestingly enough, however, we didn't choose the solemn high liturgy of our Prothonotary Apostolic pastor, the good Monsignor, with his mitre, gloves and buskins, as one might imagine might dominate the imagination of a child. Our liturgies were mimes of the everyday Mass, without choir or sermon, attended by people with perhaps a stronger focus of piety, and more time on their hands. I guess these were the only rubrics we could be sure to follow. Perhaps in the simplicity of our childish spirituality we foresaw the appropriateness of using our own English language for participation in the home setting.

Preparations for the holy event could take half an hour. Selection of the site was never a question: we used as a setting for our mass the long churchlike front foyer of the house, with its furthest section (what must have been the landing of the formal staircase in the original plan of the house) framed off from the rest of the great room by a stolid lintel of oak. This, then, was the sanctuary with its fine ebony table as the altar. On the floor in front of that table and identifying that section of the hall as its own entity was a rather large area rug of pink shag centered on the hardwood floor beyond the long gray rug of the foyer itself.

It all started one Saturday morning as we were doing household chores. That old rug did not respond very well to the vacuum sweeper, its long fibers always getting clogged in the brushes and powerful airstream of the appliance, so we took one of the large combs the girls always had on their dresser in the Pink Room and tried to tease the filaments of that floor covering into some sort of order. The results were pleasing to the eye, and it did not take long for Bobbi to come up with the notion that here was a special place, a locus perfect for the celebration of Mass.

The rest fell into line automatically. I would be the priest, since I was the oldest male. Jimmy, just starting as an altar boy, could practice that privileged service under Bobbi's careful supervision, and Maureen would be one of the ladies in the congregation. One of the goblets from our parents' silver cocktail set was perfect for the chalice, and a white Necco Wafer a fitting host. The wine would have to be red Cool-Aid, and we could decant it, along with the Lavabo (hand washing) water, from authentic cruets (just like at church!) used on special occasions in our dining room for salad dressing. We found a bell somewhere for the *Hanc Igitur* and Consecration, and with our St. Joseph Daily Missals at the ready, we could conduct a complete liturgy, although once again we were ahead of our time with use of the vernacular. The Prayers at the Foot of the Altar, however, had to remain in Latin. After all, Jimmy was practicing the responses, and I beginning to study the mysterious tongue of Latin itself. Essential parts of the Mass required the sophistication of the universal language of the Church, anyone could tell you! (Actually, these prayers were among the first medieval accretions to the mass to be dropped by the liturgical reform of Vatican II!)

If you ask whether this was a truly religious activity for us kids, I'd have to say both yes and no. Yes, because it certainly wasn't about anything else besides religion; it was an imitation of our most precious activity, carried out with all the solemnity we could muster. But no, it wasn't truly religious because we never had any idea of the presence of God at our "Mass," and we certainly weren't praying when we performed it; we were playing. It is interesting to note, however, that we didn't *pray* much at a real Mass, either. Now I may be mixing spiritualities here, and judging one period by the piety of another, but I think it important to note that Catholic spirituality in those days, at least for this child, did not emphasize much the intimacy a religious person is supposed to have with God. Key to being a good Catholic (our way of saying "being a religious person") lay in keeping the laws of God and the laws of the Church!

Consider this comparison: As a child Jesus himself, as a good Jew, prayed the Psalms daily at home, in synagogue, and when he went to the Jerusalem Temple for big feasts. Later, as an adult, he showed a life-long familiarity with these sacred Hebrew prayers and used them extensively in his public ministry. We Catholics of the 1950s prayed the rosary as our main prayer, daily if possible. Now besides the beautiful praise of the Blessed Virgin in the main prayer of the rosary, the Hail Mary, the main petition we made, fifty times a day in the fifty Hail Marys of the rosary, was to ask Mary for help at the time of our death, calling ourselves "sinners" those many times: "Pray for us sinners, now and at the hour of our death."

So, Jesus' prayers were full of praise and thanksgiving to God, along with recitation of God's saving deeds for humanity and only a few curses for enemies: "Merciful and gracious is the Lord, slow to anger... abounding in love" (Ps 103:8); "God's anger lasts but a moment, a lifetime his loving mercy" (Ps 30:6). Even the cursing Psalms helped bring anger out into the open and into prayer. We were taught to suppress anger as something always bad. As Old Testament scholar Gregory Polan says, "The Psalms take us from the heights of praise to the depths of distress with language that always gives rise to a life-giving hope." Of course, we 1950s Catholics knew that God was all good and loving toward us, but we hardly ever said it, what we said put ourselves down as sinners with a death as a terrible danger to keep ever in mind, *Dies irae. dies illa*, "The Day of wrath, that Day," we sang at the requiem mass, the black vestment mass that we had almost every weekday in the 1950s.

Well, religion for us in those days meant the practice of religion. "Attending" Mass (rather than "celebrating" it), saying the rosary, making the Stations of the Cross and fasting in Lent, giving money to the church and, to be sure, a very strict moral code, these were the major components of our Catholicism. But even our moral decisions were not made out of the love of God–well, not directly at least. We did what was right because that's what God wanted of us, since we were created "to know, love, and serve God." The presence of a loving and caring eternal Parent somehow got lost in the prescriptions of what it was that made you a Catholic. We didn't even call ourselves Christians because Protestants, who were always calling themselves "Christians," didn't have the special vocation to live out the "perfect" system of belief and practice we had. We respected them, of course, but for all we knew, they didn't even know what they had to believe—or what was a sin for that matter, because they lacked the guidance of the infallible Magisterium of our Church.

Vatican II brought Catholics more into contact once again with the teaching of Jesus as lived in the early Church, namely, with the central awareness of the loving presence of an ever-creating God. Many Catholics rejoiced to be so enriched with that deepening of our doctrine and practice. Many walked away, unfortunately, hurt and angry at having been duped for so many years into thinking themselves irreligious because they didn't—or couldn't—appreciate the externals of the religion of their childhood.

Part 4 – School

1 – Kindergarten

The first experience of going to school for Catholic kids back in those days did not usually begin in a Catholic school. Since we didn't have pre-school at Holy Rosary, I had to go to the local public school to experience it. This was Sterrett School up on Reynolds St., just a couple blocks up Lang Ave from Thomas Blvd. We walked there and back every day without the slightest fear for our safety, even though we were only five and six years old. Times have sure changed, haven't they?

Ah, but so has pre-school. Back then it was a morning of supervised playtime called Kindergarten. I mean by this that we didn't have any particularly academic exercises, but spent our time coloring and playing games with a lot of singing, quite unlike the modern instruction of pre-school children in reading and counting both in school and on public television. I don't know which is better, but I do know that "play" Kindergarten helped to prepare us for some of the social realities of "real" school pretty well.

The classroom was in the front of the building on the first floor, and it was large and very bright, having windows on two sides. It had loads of hand-colored decorations all over the walls since we didn't need any blackboard space. There were huge bins of toys and especially blocks, complemented by drawers full of crayons, chalks and drawing paper. No writing meant no need for desks, so our seating was arranged in several settings with tiny chairs and tables to match our minuscule features.

All in all, it was a very happy place, with lots of nice things to see and to hear. I don't remember my teacher at all, but she must have been very nice and able to control the kids very well, for, after the tearful beginning of the semester (a lot of the other kids cried, but not me!), there wasn't very much crying or misbehaving at all. I guess that we were having fun and already knew that being bad at school was an embarrassment to the family that would not be tolerated. In our house THE RULES did not contain any explicit sanctions for having been called out at school, but it was abundantly clear that that was never to happen.

We played and colored and sang and listened to the stories our teacher read to us. One of my favorite things to do was to build with blocks. The school had wonderful, big blocks of simple design, crude pieces fashioned from two-by-four lengths of wood, probably cut and sanded smooth in the school's woodshop, a place I would experience for myself some seven years later. They were special blocks, however, bigger and therefore more fun than anything like it you could get for Christmas, even Lincoln logs.

One day a boy in the class was crying bitterly, "My biwnding keeps fawwing dahn," he bawled. I said to him, "Let's start over. You tell me how you want to make it and I'll help you." With a child's instinctive desire to be of help, and with the immensely gratifying feeling of really being helpful to someone, I put aside my own plans, brought my blocks over, and joined in a cooperative effort which resulted in a nice construction, and one of the dearest things anybody ever said to me. "I weawwy wike you, Buddy!" came straight from the boy's heart and I knew for the first time in my life what it means to be thanked, thanked sincerely by someone who truly appreciated and actually needed your help. I can't recall the boy's name, nor did I ever see him afterward around the neighborhood as we were growing up, but he is very much in there among all the clutter in the part of my heart reserved for Thomas Blvd.

2 – Starting at Holy Rosary School

Now first grade was a completely different experience from Kindergarten. It was the start for me of seven years of important relationships at Holy Rosary Grammar School in Homewood where my mind and heart began its encounter with the great miracle of knowledge. Here also I experienced and began to understand the selflessness of the nuns who gave their lives in loving service to awaken our minds and bring us to a reflective awareness of the wonders of the world around us.

If, even in those days, some kids merely tolerated school, and a few didn't like it, I loved it! I took delight in its every aspect. Yes, going to school at Holy Rosary School was a wonderful experience, and starting out there after kindergarten at Sterrett Public School was like coming home. First of all, the school was right next to the church, the center of our spiritual lives, which meant that Holy Rosary was the place where almost everything that was most important to us came into focus. Not only did we assemble there, praying and receiving the sacraments, but our religious lives could be enhanced and informed by a school that was religion-focused.

In the school itself, there was something refined about our first grade classroom. I suppose it was the presence of blackboards (they still were black in those days and made from great slabs of slate) and the corkboards above them filled with the alphabet and many sets of numbers. There was something special in how each Sister contributed her own personal signature to her classroom. Some were pretty, some were strong and bold, and none were ever the slightest bit dirty or messy in any respect. We had an omnipresent janitor, Mr. Johnson, to make sure of that!

Sr. Mary Hugh was our first grade teacher. A big woman, she was somewhat matter-of-fact and clearly in charge of her students. It was she who introduced us to the new world of the letters of the alphabet. It's probably hard now to imagine a world without modern children's public television, with its clever cartoons sneaking across to tiny minds the names of twenty-six letters and the spelling of some simple words. But for us, the first grade was our initiation into that world of literacy and the magic of combining a few symbols to designate the words that both create and explain our culture. For us first-graders then the alphabet was what began to put us into a higher level of communication with what was around us, for no part of radio that I know of back then was geared to children, and television was in its infant stages. It was 1952, after all.

One event that sticks in my mind was my earliest experience of my human limitations, a kind of first public acknowledgement that I could make mistakes, that my performance for the world could be less than perfect, and that I would have to live with that. I think I knew that I didn't always do the right thing at home and with my friends, but nobody ever made a big deal out of it.

To have given some wrong answers in my "Think and Do" book, however, was a different matter. This was to have a record of my fallibility right in front of me. (We corrected our own books, but the thought of changing the pencil marks to the correct answers—cheating—never even entered my head.) Somehow I had gotten into my awareness a judgment that good boys and girls didn't make mistakes in school, for that surely meant that they weren't paying attention or that the error resulted from some other bad action for which one was culpable. (See, there's that Catholic guilt I was talking about!) In other words, instead of learning the important lesson of the fallibility of the human mind, I was certain that only some moral weakness could have led me to disappoint Sister, whom I was trying with all my heart to please. I don't remember how she helped me through the enormous stress and embarrassment I felt both at being wrong and at crying in public, but somehow time passed and I learned how to deal with failure without crying for everybody to see. But I still don't like to be wrong, especially when it is apparent to more than myself and anyone but the closest of confidants!

The big event of first grade, of course, was making our First Holy Communion. For this we drilled seemingly for hours on how to walk in procession in perfect formation two by two, not ahead and not behind your partner, how to genuflect in perfect unison at the sound of Sister's clicker, and then to split off into our designated pew to our designated place in that pew, there to stand, sit or kneel at the click that gave the signal. I'm sure we were given quite a bit of instruction on what the holy eucharist was and what it meant to receive our Lord in Holy Communion, but I can't remember a word of it! What we did understand was that everyone was making a big fuss over us as we took one more step into full communion (good choice of words!) with the parish as a whole. Some Catholics I know are actually angry that in Catholic school they never learned about the eucharist as the sacrament of God's love for us in Jesus, our Lord! They claim, as a matter of fact, that they didn't learn much at all about the love of God, but they did memorize the seven sacraments, the four cardinal virtues, seven gifts of the Holy Spirit, twelve fruits of same, and all the answers in the Baltimore Catechism!

Because of all the emphasis on moral correctness, discipline at Holy Rosary was never much of a problem. Would I say it was very strict there? It certainly was by some of today's standards, but we never felt it to be anything unusual. That's just the way it was at Holy Rosary, and we were very proud to be there. Take the schoolyard, for instance. Each morning, before starting the school day, we arrived, depending on our grade, at one of two fenced schoolyards, in the morning and once again after we returned from our walk home for lunch. In the yard we were allowed to chat and run and play until the first loud beep sounded over the PA system. Then every child of us stopped in our tracks, frozen in silence in the exact position we found ourselves in at that moment. Only at the second beep did we commence to move, but still in perfect silence, to form flawless ranks two by two in the designated area for one's particular class. No one ever questioned this maneuver or thought it strange; it was just what we did when the beeps sounded.

On rare occasion, usually when someone new came to school, there might be heard a whisper after the first beep or even a slight adjustment of position made, but that was quickly terminated by the Nun's Eye. Long before the deadly red dot of the laser sight from an assassin's rifle, the sisters had perfected a stare that could immobilize any child whose eye it caught: Nun's Eye! Now every nun had been outfitted with this uncanny, nearly lethal, device, and there were several masters of its use, Sr. Judith being particularly adept at its deployment. But no one could compare with the heart-stopping, silent blaze of the puissant Nun's Eye of Sr. Ann Gertrude, the principal of Holy Rosary School. Now here was a person so in charge that her very appearance outside her forbidden office bade woe to all who saw her. To my knowledge, the full potency of that merciless gaze had never been tested, because we never saw anybody walking around with a hole drilled completely through their cranium, the sure result of doubting the efficacy of that woman's withering gaze.

Second grade was where we learned to write in cursive script instead of printing everything. We practiced and tried to master the smooth, flowing ligatures of the Palmer method of handwriting. (After about forty years I returned to printing anything important I needed to jot down by hand, since my handwriting had regressed to its pre-second grade level.)

Our classroom was down, off to the side of the old gym/auditorium, a leftover from the days when Holy Rosary had its own girls' high school back in the Forties. This was before the renovations and the new gym were made after the Great Fire. Sr. Redempta was a wonderful middle-aged nun who had a way of making me feel very special when she liked my homework or performance on a test. But more than that, I'm sure that she is the first person outside the family that I ever experienced as truly loving, even though I know that I was incapable of returning such affection for a couple of years hence.

Second grade, too, was the time when you started piano lessons, if your parents encouraged you to do so. In our house we all took lessons, all five of us kids willing or not, and the half hour practice per day was closely regulated by Mom. My teacher was a retired Sister. I don't remember her name or that she was very inspiring at lessons. I found out in college that my playing wasn't very inspiring, either. And with no encouragement from my professor (but no resistance from him either!) I simply quit piano and put my music time to better use in chorus. The experience of joining a group of nearly fifty young adults making reasonably good music out of a classic cantata sticks with me to this day–but we're not talking about this day, are we? (Maybe we are!)

Anyway, music theory classes began in third grade, and I quickly mastered the theoretical part of music for beginners, learning to identify the notes of both staffs and rattle off all the key signatures, tempi and scales that are basic to our conventional Western music. In addition to music theory, participation in the school orchestra, too, started in the third grade. I was given a cello (no reason given!) and learned the elementary fingering of the first position on that instrument under the very capable direction of our zealous music teacher, Sr. Sylvia (yes, we had a whole nun just for music instruction to all the classes and for "orchestra"!).

Our practices were punctuated by the wonderful monthly visits of a Dr. Aroticus (?), a symphony violinist with infinite patience and a very clear teaching method. How we loved it when he would soar above the melody of a piece an octave higher than the others still struggling with the first position on their fiddles. The school provided instruments and biweekly practices for any student who wanted them. Oh, and as a bonus all orchestra members were taken to the Children's Concerts of the Pittsburgh Symphony, at beautiful Carnegie Hall in Oakland. The beginning I had in music at Holy Rosary clearly set a course of appreciation and enjoyment of that Muse for the rest of my life.

One thing that I regret from the fourth or fifth grade was an indiscretion that haunts me to this day. There was a girl in class who evidently had what we would call today an attention deficit problem or perhaps dyslexia, because she seemed very slow when she spoke and had great difficulty reading. In my ten-year-old estimation, she was just dumb. There's no other way to describe my opinion of the situation at the time, and what's worse, I mocked her for it. There was an advertising jingle that I parroted, using her name over and over in a derisive song I would sing when she was around. Whatever her problem, she set about solving it in a most direct way.

One day after school I noticed her a couple of times in the distance until I realized that she was trying to follow me home, evidently to complain to a higher authority. I tried to throw her off by ducking around to the alley to enter the house from the back, but to no avail. When I got into the kitchen, the front doorbell rang, and I hastened to be the first one there to answer it. Sure enough, there she was just as Mom also arrived at such an unusual ring at the door. I scooted away but within a few minutes Mom called me and I had to face whatever music was about to play.

Mom was angry at me for being so mean to a girl whose only fault was something she could not control. I was given strict orders never to tease her again. I don't remember what Mom said, but I avoided that girl and kept my mouth shut when she read or recited in class from then on. Children can be so mean to other children until they are brought to realize the hurt they cause. That girl may have been slow, but she was far from stupid in her handling of this insensitive boyo who Mom said might be too smart for his own good.

3 – The Sisters

Holy Rosary Grammar School was probably one of the best Catholic schools in the country in the Fifties. Of first importance was the presence and guidance of the Sisters of St. Joseph, the "Josies," as we called them. There were three class sections of grades one through four and two each for grades five to eight, each with its own classroom and, more importantly, each had its own teacher, a "Josie." In addition, we had Sr. Sylvester who did nothing but music, Sr. Ann for art, and, of course, the formidable Sr. Ann Gertude the principle, the inside of whose office you never wanted to see! (Oh, there was a housekeeper sister, too, and possibly even another one who did the cooking.)

Except for music, art and the eighth grade, the sisters didn't rotate between classes, but each sister took care of her own class, instructing in all areas. In this way, Sister (we always called them "Sister"—no "Strrs" allowed, or you heard about it!), Sister knew each student individually and very well because of the variety of settings and subjects in which that "homeroom" teacher interacted with the children. But, more than that, these were truly excellent women, whether newly professed or veteran, with a dedication to God in their religious life that shone through in their considered interaction and loving concern for each child. Oh sure, there were characters, as you will see, but I'd compare our Sisters to any group of teachers you could line up today. What they might have lacked in professional training, they more than made up for in the personal attention and genuine care they gave to each one of us. They made us very proud of going to Catholic school, and not just any Catholic school, Holy Rosary Catholic School!

The special teachers for art and music, gifted Sisters who traveled from room to room, at different times of the day and week, drew out of us kids whatever talents and sentiments lay dormant in our childhood. The wonderful Sr. Sylvia would haul that little pump organ around from room to room, teaching us to love to sing. When we would hear ourselves make wonderful noises with our voices and make that beautiful sound that only young boys and girls can create—on pitch and in rhythm—I think it brought forth something that really affected our whole lives. It certainly made me proud: my own song with my own voice!

The Sisters were young and they were old, and mostly, in-between. Sr. Mary Julius, my sixth grade teacher, was young and very beautiful. The heavy, pleated habit and the masking effect of the awesome headgear and bib the Sisters endured every day could not cloak the bloom of her figure nor the comeliness of her face. I remember remarking to myself, in my own snotty pre-teen way, that she didn't explain things in religion very well; she didn't always answer our questions to my satisfaction, but she gave us the freedom to ask genuine and meaningful questions. The sense of recognition we derived from that approval of our thoughts gave us more than any "correct" answer ever could.

One day we were decorating the classroom, probably for Easter, because we were going all out with the lilies we drew and colored on the corkboard atop the blackboards in the room. Tommy O'Malley, who was a little chunky in those days, was a newish friend I was growing to like in Altar Boys, and he was standing on tiptoes on a chair with his back to the room, pinning up the flowers and what-not at his maximum reach. I don't know what got into me, I was usually quite a calm and serious student, but I started contemplating a pin I held in my hand and was drawn ineluctably to place it somewhere within the right buttock of my corpulent and sprawling friend. Which I did. The reaction was far greater than I had expected, not having myself as yet ever experienced the effect a straightpin can have on one's gluteus maximus. But Tommy did, and the box of pins he was holding went flying over his shoulder to every part of the room. His yelp was totally unmuffled by any sense of decorum, Tommy having been taken completely by surprise at my lack of restraint. The young Sr. Mary Julius didn't know whether to spit or say a rosary, but she said not a word. When we all, including Tommy, recovered our composure, we pretended nothing had happened, quickly but quietly gathering up the pins, and then we simply went on with our tasks.

After class, Sister asked me why I had done what I did. I said that I honestly didn't know and that I never do anything like that, and certainly never would again. She said "All right, but I'm still very cross with you! Never, never do anything like that again!" And that was the end of it. That is, until Tommy O'Malley caught up with me after class. We were never very pugilistic at Holy Rosary; it was considered quite vulgar to fight and the consequences were too high when you considered that the priests would be called in and parents notified. Having thus been spared the experience of my first punch in the nose, I did have the experience, for the first time in my life, of having the epithet "sunnuvabitch" cast personally in my direction.

Before that, in the fifth grade I was in the classroom of Sr. Saint Anne, an elderly lady who had spent years as a missionary in China before the communist takeover there in the Forties. Her eyes were very weak and she always wore a thick pair of glasses with a deep rose tint, something quite unusual in those days. Rumor had it that before being expelled from that country she had been tortured by the communists, and that the many blows she received from them resulted in the attenuated condition of her eyesight. She was very, very kind and always made me feel like a special person. I carried her bookbag over to the convent for her whenever I could and she once rewarded me with the unheard of extravagance of milk and cookies in the convent's kitchen. I think she was the first adult outside of my family that I ever loved.

Sr. Oswald favored some of us students in the fourth grade. At times when the classroom decorations needed to be refurbished or altered for the season, she would assign a workbook exercise to the rest of the class and let us "good" students color-in the flowers or Easter eggs as the others plugged through the lengthy drill. I know that it was not a matter of some of us having artistic talent that accounted for the selection, because I have a complete lack of that magic in my fingers, the gift that allows one to recreate reality with the merest smudges of chalk or carbon. I gained something of an insight into technique, however, when Sister showed us how to shade the leaves of certain daffodils we were making by simply using different shades of crayon at different points within the leaf. I realized definitively, however, that I had no ability at drawing, because I completely failed to get the proper curve into a daffodil leaf when I was given a tryout earlier with those who were chosen to sketch the flowers themselves.

One day in class I pushed the envelope of being one of the "smart" students too far. We were reading Bible history, a subject which gave us a familiarity with the many wonderful tales of the Old Testament, but which completely lacked any interpretation of them or application to our life as a "People of the Book." We were reading about the accession of Joshua (see the Book of Numbers, chap. 27), and Sister kept pronouncing the name of Eleazer, the priest that consecrated Joshua, as "*El-ay-AH-zer.*" That didn't sound right to me, so I looked up the pronunciation in the back of the book where phonetic transcriptions were given of most names. Well, it was clearly marked "El-ee-AY-zer," so I raised my hand, was recognized, and politely said "I think that name is pronounced 'El-ee-AY-zer.'" She said, "No, it's 'El-ay-AH-zer.'" I got up from my desk, went up to her at the front of the room, and showed her the pronunciation given in the book. "See," I said, "It's 'El-ee-AY-zer.'" There was no doubt but that I was correct, but I saw the flash of her eye and caught the slap of her hand right across my face, with the words, "Don't ever contradict the teacher! Now go back to your desk and sit down!" ringing in my ear.

I did as I was told, putting my hand to my insulted cheek more to hide my shame than to soothe the flesh, which stung not so much from the blow itself as from the deep humiliation I felt. I was utterly surprised at receiving such discipline as I had never gotten before from anyone, not even my mother. No words were spoken in parting that day after class and the privileged relationship, crayons and all, continued for the rest of the year. I knew she was wrong, wrong both in her (latinizing, as I now understand) pronunciation of the name and in the way she handled her embarrassment at being caught out in a mistake, but it never occurred to me to make appeal to a higher authority or to question her right to the action in question. I still wouldn't!

I shouldn't end my notes on the Sisters on this sour one, but the stories of seventh and eighth grade have their place only at the conclusion of our story, even though they include a couple more very interesting interactions with the good Sisters. So I'll just switch to the next segment of my story, one about summer camp, assuring you that my love for the Sisters has never wavered and that my gratitude to them for starting me off in the right directions in many areas of life is profound. I know that I would not have developed my love of learning in the same way, nor would my ability to be thankful for gifts so freely given have begun so early in my life.

4 – Camp Rosary

One of the things I really enjoyed as a kid was a two-week stay at a summer camp called Camp Rosary. Yes, it was founded from Holy Rosary Parish, created under the direction of Fr. James Logue, and administered by him even when he was transferred out of Holy Rosary to be pastor of St. Thomas More Parish in Bethel Park. When Fr. Logue retired, the Catholic Diocese of Pittsburgh saw its great value and changed it over to a CYO (Catholic Youth Organization) administration, but all that happened only later in the late 1960s.

Going to camp was for many of us the first time we were ever away from home. It was the beginning of the many signs of trust that my parents so often gave me that grew my independence to do many things, including leaving home at eighteen for Saint Vincent College and one year later entering the monastery for a very happy life as a Benedictine monk. As it turns out, my vocation to Saint Vincent came about when I was trusted to leave home for summer camp at just 15 years old, to work as a lifeguard at that camp still controlled by Fr. Logue and his staff.

But back to my first summer stay at camp as a ten-year-old: this was where I really got to know the McGannon boys, who lived an otherwise prohibitively distant two blocks from the Alley and my small circle of friends. It was the summer of 1956, when the camp was at its former location, an old CCC campsite that is now the public beach at the lake in Laurel Hill State Park, just an hour away from Pittsburgh. We were the youngest kids in camp, esp. Georgie, who was more than a year younger than Danny and I, but that didn't stop us from having a great time together. We were cabin mates along with five other boys in a log cabin where I don't think we ever got sleep before one o'clock in the morning for all our laughing and joking. We didn't worry at all about Georgie being picked on by the other boys. He was pretty hefty, like his Dad, and more than able to hold his own in a pillow fight or minor altercation.

The counselors liked us and sort of made us their mascots. That first year Bingo O'Malley, a seminarian from Pittsburgh, was in charge of the unit, and we could tell that he was really looking out for us, but he really surprised us one night at the great campfire. Bingo had primed us all day, saying that he was going to tell some scary stories that night. He did not disappoint us. After the campfire songs died down and our eyelids began to droop, Bingo laid out the rules for ghost story listening. "No flashlights," he said. "If I see a single beam of light, that's the end of the story. And no talking or trying to scare anybody. That just ruins the story for all of us." He was very adamant on this point. "Let's all be very quiet and get into a mood to really scare ourselves. It's more fun that way." With the obvious seriousness of his intent, we all settled down in our places, I on a log just a few feet away from the master storyteller.

The tale started out with two English boys whose parents were tragically killed in an auto accident. The boys quickly departed from home lest they be put into an orphanage, since they were not close to any relatives. The older, protective, brother had heard his parents speak of their strange grandmother who lived out in the county near a small town not very far away. They were able to hop a freight train in the right direction and jumped off at the outskirts of the village as soon as they saw the signpost. Of course, it was the middle of the night. The older boy remembered some vague directions and soon enough they happened upon a broken-down house that fit the description of their grandmother's old place. They quietly approached the porch and knocked on the door. "Anybody ho-ome?" they squeaked. There was no answer, of course—this is a ghost story—but the door creaked open with the force of the knocking. As they entered the sitting room, they caught sight of an incredibly old hag with a grotesquely withered face and long black fingernails. "Come in, boys," she croaked, "You must be very tired." She bade them go straight up and take the two rooms at the top of the stairs. The older boy protested that they would only need one room … but the old woman insisted that they accept her hospitality and each have their own room.

Well, now that the boys were separated, the story could go on with some horrible, evil creature coming into the younger boy's room, et cetera, et cetera, building suspense until the boy woke up with a scream, exquisitely performed by Bingo himself and scaring me two feet straight up off that log with a scream of my own. That was fun, and we giggled far into the night back at our cabin, reliving the experience, trying to scare each other, tussling and hitting with pillows until the counselors came up to yell at us, "Go to sleep. It's one o'clock in the morning!"

The next year we heard one about a werewolf from Mr. John DiRobbio, the Camp Director himself, this time complete with the souvenir sword that John had actually struck the werewolf with himself! Even at eleven years old I knew that the red stains on the sword were a bunch of hooey, but I sure did jump a full six feet back when John made that werewolf spring out at us at the climax of the story.

In the year that followed, we had grown to love those awful, cold and rainy hikes and overnights out of camp. With only an ancient Adirondack for shelter over your head and a quilty sleeping bag between you and the often fifty-degree August nights up on Laurel Mountain, we fell asleep only because we were exhausted from a full day's hike. But the most fun of all were with the massive all-Unit war games we played back at camp. Our favorite was "Capture the Flag." In this most serious piece of play, the Units and their counselors squared off against each other in two great armies who strategized to grab the flag other side protected behind enemy lines. Needless to say they guarded that symbol mightily and there were a lot of skinned knees, and even some bruised ribs and bloody noses when two of the bigger boys got out of control on one nearly successful foray. But it was mostly great fun, a lot of whooping and hollering, with immense pride going to the winners. To make it more fair we youngsters were always teamed up with Unit 3, where the biggest boys of the camp always lodged. I was really saddened in the Spring of 1959 when I thought my summer camp days were over. We were moving to Buffalo that August, and Camp Rosary was just too far away from Buffalo for a thirteen-year-old.

Fast forward two years after leaving Pittsburgh, the place of my happy childhood, when my love for all my Pittsburgh friends became too great, I pleaded with my folks to be allowed to return to Camp Rosary for my first summer job. I was only fifteen, but, as I had kept up with some of the counselors, and because Dad talked to Jim Hannan, a good friend from his school days at Central Catholic and a board member of the camp, I was hired as "boat boy" for the summer of 1961. I returned for two more summers, and many of the wonderful occurrences of my teenage life took place there, including my first association with Benedictines as assistant to the chaplain. This is not the place, but the stories of Camp Rosary in those wonderful years of the early Sixties and of the excellent people who staffed the camp—while having the time of their lives—must someday be told.

5 – Kennywood

Kennywood. The very name sounds like fun! That institution began with a great idea at the end of the nineteenth century by the skillful entrepreneurs of one of the old private streetcar lines in town. They bought a piece of forest at the end of their Monongahela Street line and fashioned a park there so that people would use the streetcars on weekends as well as to go to work during the week. What a lovely idea, even if motivated by the dollar!

The park grew popular, and its character changed so that in fifty years it became a thriving amusement park on its site high above the Monongahela River. The view from its grand Ferris Wheel is spectacular! The park boasted a great midway and all kinds of rides for children and adults, but at the center of it all was the merry-go-round, a classic carousel, complete with its steam calliope. You could feel its vibrations when it played! The park also boasted some of the best roller coasters in the country, a colossal penny arcade, and couple of great indoor experiences like Noah's Ark and "Laughing in the Dark." They had new and wonderful circus acts every week of the summer, and along with food stands everywhere, there was a pretty good restaurant in the center of the park. Going there on school holiday was the major event of the year for us kids at Holy Rosary School.

The whole parish got involved! Volunteer mothers working with the sisters packed lunches for all of us kids for the day long festivities, brown paper bags with awful sandwiches of American cheese—even though we never had the outing on a Friday! Putting us in reach of those Kennywood hot dogs on a Friday would have constituted a near occasion of sin! Since the event was always on a school day, most of the fathers had to work and couldn't join us until the end of the day. The nuns never went, either. I guess such a fun place was considered too secular for those holy women. But I think it was because they really deserved a day off from us little whirling dervishes!

Several streetcars were commandeered, with "Special" lit up in their marquees, and at nine o'clock in the morning the entire school lined up in front of the local Carnegie Library at the streetcar stop on Hamilton Ave. There we would go on board under the supervision of some of the mothers who had martyr complexes—or no other means of getting to the park. We all set out together for a most adventurous day at one of the best amusement parks in the world at that time. Come to think of it, most of the mothers must have come along with us, but I clearly remember that my gang did not want any adult with them on the "rides." Yes, that's what we called them, for the ones we liked were all thrillers that spun you, turned you upside down or threw you up and down, from side to side in sharp turns at breakneck speeds.

Kennywood opened up a new ride every year. I think the one we enjoyed most was the "Rotor," a spinning cylinder whose floor fell out as soon as you were glued to its cushioned inner surface by centrifugal force. In our last year in Pittsburgh they unveiled the "Rock 'n Roll," a tortuous Ferris wheel-like contraption whose gondolas not only went up and around on the great wheel, but spun freely on their axels—the whole way around if you were crazy enough to pull hard on the big ring handle inside your protective basket. Yeow! Just thinking of it now makes me nauseous! I remember I didn't like it very much even when I was a youngster!

The real rides at Kennywood, 'oh—that's the way we said "though" back then—the real reason why any kid over ten came to Kennywood, were the rollercoasters. These days there are all kinds of nasty metal scare-the-life-out-of-you, looping and twisting cars on tracks, even at Kennywood, but back then, and still the pride of the park, there were three wooden coasters, and they were already long in the tooth when we grew tall enough to ride them.

First, and the least scary of all, was the "Racer." This amusement had two long cars running on separate, but parallel tracks, up, down and around what seemed like a half mile of track. The participants were immediately locked in deep competition as we rounded every turn, cascaded down every hill, screaming with delight as your car passed the other, taunting and jeering, only to be passed up on the next turn with the other car's occupants squealing their own gibes and pointing their mocking fingers.

The next instrument of gleeful intorsion was called the "Jackrabbit," so named after its stomach-lifting double dip from atop the highest point in the park. The whole ride was conceived as prelude and postlude to this heart-stopping taste of real danger. A few innocuous hills and turns brought you around to the slow climb up to the brink of that suicidal chute: "Clink, clink, clink . . ." you would climb, seemingly forever, until you thought you could stand it no longer, coming almost to a standstill as you began the turn at the crest. Then you gained a tiny bit of momentum rounding the 180 degrees of the curve, and, of a sudden, you saw before you the enormous chasm into which you were about to plummet. For not only was your car at the top of the ride's very high scaffolding but stretched out below was a deep ravine into which you were about to plummet.

Finally, coming off the final part of the turn with a modicum of speed, the bottom dropped out and your stomach lifted up to your throat as you roared down the short but very steep first hummock. Then your tummy slammed flat as you hit the level part when it floated up again as your lap came up hard against the restraining bar in the car's next freefall. Down the long stretch you shot at immense speed till you bottomed out, straining with all your might to keep your chin from sagging onto the deck. A terrible reverse twist at top speed jerked the cars back around, and with a final high G-force lifted you up to the starting platform where you screeched to a halt still holding your breath. With unsure legs and an awed silence you made your exit, panting and holding on to the rails as you eyed up the line and calculated how long it would take till you could ride it again!

The third roller coaster was called the Pippin. This was the only ride in the park I ever remember being too small to ride. When I had grown sufficiently, I must admit I found it disappointing after the rather mild ride but high-level competition of the Racer and the dramatic contortions of the Jackrabbit. The Pippin had the longest (but straight-down) drop, from up high in the scaffolding down past ground level into a great valley where a dark tunnel covered the sharp turnaround that brought you to the end of the ride. For all that, we were taking its big hill "no-hands" long before we dared try it on the Jackrabbit.

Other rides, such as "Laughin' in the Dark," one of those dark, funhouse rides (the model for our back hall "funhouse" at 6928), were good for starters, and we never missed the absolutely antique "Noah's Ark," with its worn-out animations and famous air jet for lifting the ladies' dresses. We never "wasted our time" at the penny arcade at the silly rubber ball bowling, much less at the ancient flipping card animated picture viewers—nor did we have any money for them. And I have no memory of ever actually riding the famous merry-go-round until I was over thirty. We did pause from our breakneck rollercoaster passion once every trip to rent a rowboat in the big pond that surrounded the park's main stage. From there we could watch close-up the arial artists ply their ropes and swings overhead. I once had a man shot out of a cannon come flying high across my bow.

Every year at the outing, at exactly five o'clock oddly enough (unchanging dinnertime at 6928), we would meet Mom and the newly arrived Dad—at the Merry-Go-Round, of course. After hellos and a breathless debriefing, we would proceed to the big restaurant at the center of the park. There we would first meet with Bill Stagg, the manager of the restaurant who was friends with our parents. As they chatted, we kids would be on pins and needles waiting to see how many complimentary tickets Mr. Stagg would slip to our Dad. This wad of coupons he always produced insured our limitless enjoyment all evening of even the "big" rides that consumed four and even five tickets at a gulp.

We filed inside with Mr. Stagg leading the way to a big round table where Dad ordered a full dinner of meat, mashed potatoes, vegetables and a green salad, exactly like at home! It was more fun than home, though, because we always got milkshakes to drink and most of all because it was eating "out." We took our time and didn't rush, enjoying each other's company and sharing our hair-raising experiences of the day, and all the goofy things that happen to happy kids set free at a fine amusement park. Besides, we had to rest up for a full evening's fun yet to come.

But can you imagine going out to a restaurant and ordering the usual fare and not something special, like Italian or seafood? I guess things were simpler back then when order and security triumphed at the cost of adventure. Actually, hardly anyone other than Italian Americans ate Italian food at home (I'm not counting Chef Boyardee, of course. We kids really loved that canned ravioli!). And there were precious few Italian restaurants in those days! I recall our pastor Msgr. Carlin's famous epithet for the meals he was forced to consume on pilgrimage to the Holy City of Rome: "Food unfit for human consumption!" was his assessment of all manner of pasta. Just imagine: there was not a single pizza parlor in town back then!

The piece de resistance at Kennywood's restaurant was not any of the food, not even the delicious ice cream cake we always had for dessert. No, it was seeing the priests, all at a large table, dressed in regular clothes. Well, there was not much "regular" about them. Sure, most of them had on the regulation shiny black pants, badly in need of pressing. But the shirts they wore could stop a locomotive at full steam! Bright red and lime green were rarely seen on grown men in those days, but among those garish outfits Fr. Lackner's navy blue chemise with white polka dots took the cake. I remember one of the waitresses we knew saying that you could always tell the priests on school picnic day by those outrageous clothes they wore.

Wonderful times, simple pleasures! What fun we had with Mom and Dad in the evening on the big rocket swings, target shooting, walking around eating candied apples—I never liked the cotton candy. They must have liked being there, too, because I never remember crying because we had to leave early. In fact, I never remember the ride home!

6 – Fight!

The big rival to Holy Rosary School in many ways was Sacred Heart in Shadyside. Their beautiful neo-Gothic church was the only Catholic peer to ours in the city, outside of St. Paul's cathedral, of course. The rival school, taught by a force of Charity nuns equal in number to our Josies, was probably as good. But the kicker was that many of the Catholic families of Point Breeze, much of which was within the territorial boundaries of Holy Rosary Parish, preferred to send their children to the "better neighborhood," Shady Side they thought, even though the parish is actually in East Liberty ("*ee-SLI-bər-dee*" to us natives). The basketball game that year turned out to be a double win for Sacred Heart and quite a disgrace for us. Here's what happened.

The details of the game are unimportant and less than memorable. Suffice it to say that our team was completely dominated by the better players of the rival school, and they won easily with no misconduct or poor sportsmanship that I saw. There was no taunting or other provocation on their part when they won, but after the game some of our players decided they needed some kind of a victory, even if it was of a sordid variety. Big Randolf Jones, a sixteen-year-old student who wasn't even on the basketball team, was waiting outside the visitors' locker room for the big, good-looking captain and high scorer of Sacred Heart's team. When that hapless lad exited the facility he walked straight into an angry Randolf who tried to pick a fight with him. When that didn't work, Randolf "sucker-punched" the boy, his glasses still on, and produced a nasty cut on his cheek. The jock tried to defend himself, but that was all the signal Randolf needed to go to work on him. He hit him hard several times, but the sizable fourteen-year-old would not go down.

It was at this point that I saw something that disgusted me to the point that this ninety-pounder was almost idiotic enough to intervene. An unnamable squat, yet tough, eighth grader, who could never think to engage the big visitor in a "fair" fight, moved in to get a piece of the action and, I suppose, the bragging rights in the vanquishment of the opponents' leader. As the bedazzled visitor reeled out and away from one more of Randolf's frightening punches, the coward came up on the side, out of line of sight and caught the bigger boy with a wallop to his undamaged eye. What disgusted me most was that he was wearing a big ring on his right hand, a "street fight ring," I guess, because it caught the boy under the eye and tore the skin nastily. Ugh! That might have been the lowest type of behavior I have ever seen in real life.

Fr. Spelman appeared out of nowhere and stopped the unfair attack immediately. Nobody, not even Randolf in the heat of combat, dared disobey or contradict a priest, and especially not the burley Fr. Spelman. We all disappeared instantaneously, not having had to be told to "break it up and go home." But Fr. Spelman was a good detective and had caught an eyeful of what was happening and who was present even as he fulminated against the enraged brawler and his bewildered opponent.

The next day Father called us in, one by one, to find out exactly what had happened. I guess he had already figured out that the conspiracy was to punish the leader of the team that had embarrassed us so on the court, but he didn't show any knowledge of the cowardly intervention of Mr. Squat. I had all the normal reluctance to "squeal" on a fellow student that any youngster learns from the movies, but did not hesitate for an instant to inform on the pigeon-hearted actions of that disgrace to Holy Rosary! The idiot bragged about using his "street fight ring" the next day and showed some of his cronies some blood on it. Severe and equally punitive action was taken against both the offenders (obviously I was not the only one offended by the cowardly conduct of that truant interloper), and we never heard about the episode again.

Whether we were afraid to talk about that embarrassing example of the worst Homewood could provide I can't say that I remember, but we were all ashamed to our marrow of such obvious taking advantage and tried to put it out of our minds. I have never been graced with such a gift of forgetfulness and I still marvel at how good families can instill any kind of violent vindictiveness in their children. I am strongly against harsh physical punishment for anyone, child or adult, but I know that I would have been severely tested in that resolve, if I had been the parent of that fatherless boy.

7 – The Trip to New York

One of the really cool things Dad did for me when I was a kid was to take me along with him on a business trip to New York City after school had ended. This was the nicest twelfth birthday present a boy could receive: to visit New York City with his Dad! I didn't ask for it. Dad just came up with the idea one day. I think it's an example of how THE RULES paid off. You see, Dad knew that I would do what and only what he said I could do, even by myself in the greatest city in the world. I also think he realized that if he had waited a couple of years, the teenager would have presented him with a different set of concerns in the same situation.

One warm Sunday after Church and a quick breakfast, Mom dropped us off at the recently constructed Greater Pittsburgh Airport. She said goodbye and have-a-good-time, and left Dad and me to share an experience that I will never forget. We arrived with plenty of time before take-off, and Dad explained all the features that TWA touted about our glistening new Super Constellation aircraft. I remember how strikingly modern the three-lobed tail assembly appeared along with its four ponderous and roaring engines, as we walked out and up the outdoor gangway to board the great machine.

The flight itself was uneventful once the thrill of take-off was over, it being my first airplane ride. I noticed how lovely the stewardesses were and how courteous they were to me. I think they had figured out what my obviously on-a-business-trip Father was treating me to, and decided to add to the pleasure and excitement of my experience. "Would you like a magazine, sir?" a pretty blond queried. "Here is your lunch. Now what would you like to drink, sir?" asked the tall brunette. Were they following a stricter set of guidelines for flight service back then? Or was it that I just wasn't used to adults treating a child so politely? Anyway, it worked. It felt like a big deal, you know, a kid being recognized like that!

When we landed we went straight to baggage (Carry-on was not a big thing yet!), picked up our suitcases, and jumped into a cab bound for Manhattan. We arrived at the Taft Hotel, in those days a nice, businessman-type accommodation. Our room had one of those special doors with a compartment that opened on either side for clothes to be cleaned or pressed overnight. I was excited to be staying for the first time in a hotel room, but we quickly freshened up and went out on the streets of New York!

We were right in the center of Manhattan: the hotel was on West 50th St., so we walked down Broadway to Times Square, then over on 42nd St. with all the movie houses, and turned up 9th Ave. on our way to … Mama Leone's for dinner. Oh, what a delight that was! I had never had spaghetti that good before. After a great dessert we wended our way slowly back to the hotel and I fell asleep as soon as I hit the pillow. So much excitement, so many new things.

I got up in the morning quite refreshed by a dreamless sleep. We went down to breakfast and Dad had to leave to see his client. He gave me some money for lunch and told me to be careful in traffic and to meet him back here at the hotel at four o'clock. Can you imagine today letting a twelve-year-old kid roam around New York City all day on his own?

Map in hand, I walked over to Fifth Ave. and there was St. Patrick's Cathedral! I had no sooner knelt down inside when a priest came over to me and asked if I knew how to serve Mass. I said, "I sure do." Remember: in those days there was no concelebration yet, and every priest was expected to say his own Mass, even privately, every day. And with that he disappeared for a minute or two and came out of the sacristy dressed for Mass, carrying a chalice and two cruets. I served him at one of the side altars, pleased as could be at having this great memory of this New York trip. I thought, "Won't my friends be envious of me serving mass at St. Patrick's Cathedral!"

After that I walked around Rockefeller Center marveling at the scope of it, the great Prometheus sculpture, the gardens, what a wonderful way to spend a warm afternoon in June! I was back at the hotel, ready and waiting for Dad who arrived right on time, four o'clock sharp. We took the subway down to 33rd St. at Fifth Ave. and entered the Empire State Building. I knew I was in for a thrill when we got into the express elevator that went straight up without a stop. We came out on the observation deck and I was not disappointed. We looked in every direction and Dad pointed out buildings and sights of interest. When I was pondering what would happen if you dropped a penny to the street below, we looked at each other knowing that we were ready to descend, for stomachs were growling.

We had a nice meal at, was it Lindie's?—or has my imagination filled in this part of the story? Anyway, Dad had tickets to see the Rockettes at Radio City Music Hall right nearby on 6th Ave. They were spectacular! I had never seen a stage show of this size and with such dancing precision—not to mention how pretty they were, net-stockinged legs prancing in perfect unison! There followed some newsreels and other informative film shorts. This was a great evening for me and I talked excitedly to Dad the whole short walk back to the hotel!

Next morning we were up early. After breakfast we went to the pier in Battery Park for the ferry out to the Statue of Liberty. This was a very scenic boat ride, of course, for the view of the skyline of the City, and for the famous immigrants' view of the Statue as they arrived at the land of freedom. I marveled at the size of the Statue herself, and the whole experience of the Island, climbing up the stairs inside and viewing all around through the windows in the crown. Marvelous! You couldn't go up into the torch anymore, but it was just great to see so much from the viewpoint we had. After this event we were done in New York. I was exhausted from so much input. After we had lunch we checked out and got in a cab for the airport. I don't even remember the trip home in the plane. I probably slept the whole way but with a big smile on my face.

8 – Finishing Up at Holy Rosary

Seventh grade at Holy Rosary started a new phase in my education. Not that I went to a new school, but I was beginning a change of mental gears from childish memorization to the beginnings of thinking about things academic and the rudiments of logical analysis. That's a rather pedantic way of putting it, but I can tell you that this boy became fascinated with stepping back from just passing my eyes over the page to beginning to break apart the sentences, looking up words I didn't know, and just enjoying a pleasant turn of phrase for its own sake. Now, of course, since I was destined to become an academic, a teacher in a graduate school of theology for over a hundred semesters now, it's probably not all that remarkable that I started on that track early. Perhaps this why they call it "middle school" in seventh grade.

At any rate, I was ready for some more meaty fare than I had received so far in school, and my desire was answered on two fronts: Sr. Judith's grammar course on diagramming was wonderful! Discovering the logic behind our English language, how words actually needed to follow known patterns to make sense, was an overwhelming insight for me and the seat of a fascination that stays with me even now—or maybe moreso now! But in addition to the delight of diagramming sentences, I was advanced into the eighth-grade math course. I can't for the life of me remember what the difference was in the math problems we learned to attack in that class, but it must have been significant for such an unusual thing in those days before AP math.

It was at this time, too, that a love of reading kicked in, richly nourished by our local branch of the Carnegie Library. I was advised to read the classics Tom Sawyer and Huckleberry Finn and enjoyed them very much, but I really devoured The Hardy Boys and even a couple of Nancy Drew mysteries. This process flowed freely into my high school literary critical reading in English class with some excellent diocesan priests as teachers—but my high school days in a minor seminary are beyond the scope of this book and something I'd never want to write about.

So now back to Holy Rosary and the seventh grade: Leevan Davis was a seventh grader whom I had grown to like, one of the very few African-American children we had in our school, or that I knew in Homewood itself, for that matter. Leevan was a very nice boy, very intelligent and well-behaved. We sat across from each other in Sr. Judith's class and shared comments or compared our work those times when Sister allowed discussion in her very strict class. One day we had a disagreement about something (I don't remember what) but the thing somehow escalated to strong words and some abrupt gestures that resulted in Leevan dropping his pencil or ruler. When he leaned over to pick it up off the floor he brushed my desk with his head on the way back up. My immediate reaction was a gesture that I will never forget and that embarrasses me to this day. I wiped off the edge of the desk with my hand as if he had somehow sullied the thing when his hair touched it! He saw the move and understood it instantly for the rank prejudice that it betrayed. We never spoke much after that, but then again, I wasn't in seventh grade much longer.

That Fall of 1958 was when we found out that the family was going to move to Buffalo, a terrific offer that Westinghouse made Dad that he couldn't refuse. It was one of the first times I remember Mom and Dad actually consulting us kids. I said that I didn't mind because I planned to go away from home to Minor Seminary at the Josephinum in Ohio for high school anyway. Monsignor was already trying to teach me Latin on Saturday mornings. Evidently Dad had discussed the move with Monsignor, for the next thing I knew, I was to be promoted, in the middle of the seventh grade, to the middle of the eighth grade! Here's the way I found out:

One day, Sr. Judith was discussing some point of grammar with the class from her usual spot about four feet in front of my front row desk. I wasn't paying much attention to her because Paul Hannon had gotten hold of my hand underneath his desk (where Sister couldn't see). He was mercilessly digging his thumbnail into the knuckle of my thumb which he had grabbed probably while I was trying to torture him from the front. I couldn't maneuver very well and still not be seen by Sister, and I couldn't get any leverage because of the way that devil torqued my hand behind me. When the pain grew unbearable I gave up on patience, turned round and hauled off with my free left hand, achieving contact with Paul's shoulder with fair impact. He yelped more with shock than pain, and Sister asked, "What are you two doing?" I could feel how red my face was becoming, and just then, over the loudspeaker came the words, "Lee Maloney, please come to the principal's office immediately." The thing had eyes! We always thought the nuns had preternatural gifts of observation, and here was proof of it! It wasn't until I arrived at the office and Sister Ann Gertrude started talking to me about moving into eighth grade that I realized her paging me had nothing to do with what had just happened in the classroom. Saved by the bell! (or at least by the same system that sounded the bell for the change of class periods).

Skipping a grade from the middle of seventh into the middle part of eighth grade, Sister announced to me, was something Monsignor himself had proposed so that I could graduate from Holy Rosary before we moved to Buffalo. Who knew what kind of schools they had in that far off land? Sister pointed out that I was already taking my math classes in the superior grade, and she felt I would be able to handle the rest of the material all right. As it turned out, the academic material was no problem, but what about all the other things that go on in the eighth grade?! Like this little twelve-year-old teacher's pet being accepted into the very closed circle of pubescent boys who were the lords of the school since they were the graduating class of 1959? Well, Monsignor had spoken!

The first few days in the new classroom were ones of a tolerant but very cool reception. Sr. Ligouri had told the class, my friend Jimmy

Cusick informs me, that I, Lee Maloney, would be joining the eighth-grade class because, "Lee is evidently too smart for seventh grade!" To top it all off, Jimmy tells me that I showed up the first day wearing a bow tie! After very few days, the problem came to a head when we had to walk up to Sterrett School for "Shop" class. We didn't have a workshop facility of our own at Holy Rosary, such unacademic superfluities being deemed unworthy of that refined institution. So on Thursday afternoons all the eighth-grade boys were required to march up to Sterrett School on Reynolds Street for instruction in carpentry. On my first day of said class I found myself walking just ahead of Jimmy (before we became friends!) and his buddies, the controlling group of the eighth-grade class. I was not walking ahead of the others on purpose; they were staying an unfriendly thirty feet away, making it clear that I was definitely not a part of their group.

It didn't take long for hostilities to begin. Jimmy, the ringleader of that tight knot of boys, was a rather diminutive, but very feisty lad. I quickly assessed that I might master him in a tussle, but there was no way I was going to face down the rest of the gang. Jimmy began, "What's the teacher's pet going to do in shop class? Do you think he knows what a hammer's for?" They had, in fact, already been going to "Shop" since before Christmas and were therefore way ahead of me in the projects they were doing. I don't know exactly what I responded, but knowing I was in a lose-lose situation, I put on my best smile and said something like, "I hope you guys can show me what to do."

Perceiving a slight thaw in their frosty visages, I continued the subterfuge with a whining, "I never took a class in woodworking." I was skirting the truth here, disavowing the knowledge I had of carpentry from the many hours I spent with Dad working around our house. I refrained, with some difficulty, from bragging that our home workshop was surely almost as complete as whatever they might have at Sterrett School, while stifling the temptation to point out that what we had at home by way of tools and equipment was probably more than any of them had ever seen outside of Shop class. At times, our superior economic position made me feel rather superior to my less affluent friends at Holy Rosary. I regret that very much, but, for lack of a deeper spirituality, our neighborhood, our maid, and our Buick made me feel like that.

By some miracle, Jimmy relented and condescended, "I'll help you. We're so far along on this project that you'd never catch up by yourself!" Now I'm sure that fourteen-year-old Jimmy Cusick never said that, but they were words to that effect, the effect being that I was accepted, provisionally, into the inner sanctum of the coolest boys in the eighth grade, the lords of Holy Rosary School. And it paid off big-time later on!

The seventh-grade class bully, whose name I have conveniently forgotten, had been on a rampage with me at the time. It all started back in fifth grade, I think, when he somehow started a fight between me and my friend Richie Sauerwein. Richie was smaller than me and I quickly got him down on the ground under me. I was struggling to keep him down, not even thinking of punching him, when I came to my senses and said to myself, "What are you doing. Richie is your friend!" I let him up and quickly disappeared into the school, supposedly looking for the bathroom.

The next episode with Mr. Bully was more serious. He said he could show me something really cool if I let him take my arm, loose as could be, and do something with it. He grabbed my hand and jerked down with all his might. I saw stars in my shoulder, if that is possible! Oh, did that hurt! "Why would a kid do something like that" was my only thought, as I held back the tears from the awful pain. It hurt all day and was sore the next. I happened to mention it to the guys (my new eighth grade cronies) and Pudgy got mad. "That's not right," he growled, and the next day he smacked Mr. Bully all over the schoolyard. I think he had had other interactions with him and was just looking for a reason to exert his superior strength (and certainly size!) upon the luckless fellow. Mr. Bully never bothered me again.

By way of response, the bully prevailed upon his ally, one Randolf Jones, to redeem his honor and secure the future against any further aggression on the part of our Pudgy friend. Now Randolf was that transfer student who must have been sixteen years old, who evidently had some problems, since he had remained so long in grammar school. Whatever his relationship was with Mr. Bully, he was certainly two times the toughest and most streetwise kid at our school. The very next day, as we were gathering after lunch around the side entrance to school (out of sight of the nuns and the rectory), Randolf walked up to Pudgy. Within a few seconds, the older boy hit the totally outclassed Pudgy twice, "jacked him up," and dropped him on his back right on the curb! I never saw such an ugly action in my life! The whole encounter took but five seconds and Pudgy lay on the ground, seriously hurt. A nun appeared out of nowhere and we all scrambled out of sight. Merely witnessing such an event, we felt, was enough to get us expelled, or at least some other serious punishment.

Randolf did not show up at school again, this having been now the second (that I know about) infraction of the school code about fighting, and certainly a grave one. I suppose he was transferred to the public school in our district. As for Pudgy, when he came into school the next day his face was badly bruised. He was immediately told to go home, for such was the intolerance shown at our school at the results of misconduct even on somebody else's account. The whole incident was quickly forgotten once Randolf was gone and we got back to our normal children's interactions.

Back in my new eighth grade classroom I got some static from Sr. Alphonse Liguori who evidently had excellent vision with those coke bottle bottom glasses she wore. You see, I didn't realize that just because I couldn't see under my desk when I was sitting in it didn't mean that she couldn't from her viewpoint from the front of the room. At that time in my young life I was experiencing some new developments within the precincts of my pants pockets, evidently in an excessive amount for Sister. She gave me some enigmatic caution that what she observed me doing was wrong and should stop. It took a while to get what she was talking about, and then I put two and two together, namely realizing that what went on under my desk was not all as private as I had assumed.

I don't want to conclude with these negative episodes that might efface all the wonder of learning and sheer gift of the budding friendships I had at Holy Rosary. I relate them because they happened and remain lodged in my memories of those days. School ended with me receiving the high scoring report card that I usually got, but then all efforts at 6928 turned to the great task of packing and labeling the contents of that big house into boxes for a very large moving van. The furniture alone would have made a mighty load for the movers, but we boxed up and moved almost all the free-standing stuff that graced our old digs.

Once in Buffalo, thirteen-year-old Buddy was left in charge of the movers as Mom and Dad went to close on the house. When they got back they found that I did just as they asked me to: whatever wasn't marked for a specific room went down to the basement—which by the time the unloading was finished had become completely impenetrable, stacked floor to ceiling with all the extra junk that had nowhere to go in our spacious, but not gargantuan, new home. So much for putting old things into new wineskins.

Time and distance have erased most of the bonds that I made with the people at Holy Rosary in those early, but quite formative years. I think it's true that one's lasting friends are usually those made during the college years, when the values and concerns of adult life truly begin to impact upon a person. I know that this is true at least for me, but I count my childish days at Holy Rosary as some of the happiest and most seminal in my life. I know that I was made ready for a very happy scholastic life in the prep seminary I entered for high school when we moved to Buffalo in the summer of 1959, just after my thirteenth birthday and completion of eighth grade at Holy Rosary, according as the good Monsignor had wanted. That was the end of the Pittsburgh part of my story, the final part of my innocent, prepubescent physical and emotional development, and the conclusion of the time period of this memoir!

EPILOGUE

As I revisit these stories for the I-don't-know-how-many-eth time, I am struck by how happy we were back then. We lived a straightforward, simple and authentic life with minimal pretensions and a good dose of reality. I see now how prosperous we were then in North Point Breeze, and that it contributed to our particular brand of happiness. I've seen happiness among the very poor, in Africa and in Brazil, and ours was a different kind. We were safe. We didn't have the usual Pittsburgh porch watch culture, but we did have people who paid attention to what was going on—usually very little—in the area. We didn't worry about what we would do the next day. All the material necessities of life were guaranteed by the adequate incomes of our households. We were protected by the police radio car that was almost always somewhere in the neighborhood, and by our own fire station up on Penn Ave. We were supported by so many others who pastored, taught, and otherwise cared for us.

We had easy access to stores of all kinds nearby, but not too near, to cause traffic jams and unsightly parking lots. The streets of our neighborhood were usually quiet. Heck, we even rode our sleds down Murtland Ave. in the winter with just one kid down on Thomas to keep us safe. There was just the right amount of pressure to maintain your property properly, because it was already of fine design and individuality, and that made each street quite interesting in its own way. Our population was just a bit diverse, Catholics, Protestants, mostly Presbyterian, and Jews, but all of us very white, and of course, all able to sustain the lifestyle of the neighborhood.

The real questions for me are: Is it even possible for everyone to live in such freedom and security? Wouldn't it be grand for all children grow up in a safe and protective atmosphere as we did? I realize that we are very far from such an ideal, but is it something that we should strive for? Or is prosperity and peace in life always at the expense of those less fortunate? I am convinced that the New Testament teaches, for example in the Feeding of the Four/Five Thousand, that there is always enough to go around if only people share. Is it worth trying to convince people that that is the truth and that today's Numero Uno philosophy is false, and just leads to further alienation and its concomitant violence. I'd sure like to try it!

I started to take notes on each episode, on the point of it, that is, why I remembered the event or why I thought it was important to mention, but I quickly realized that to try to sum up our life back then might only result in some trite sounding, perhaps even sentimental, nosegays. So I present the stories as true, and as entertainment, and I leave them to the reader for judgment. I hope they can generate some genuine and constructive conversations.

Who knew a house could be so important?
How are mere bricks a symbol of one's
        whole young life?
That house IS my childhood.

Sun drenched yellow bricks
        hold and reflect the incredible love
        that bound us as children
        to parents, to each other, to church.
It molded our dreams, unleashed our fantasy,
        forged our strength.

Walls and halls, window seats and pocket doors,
        porch swing, leaded windows.
Indoors from basement to attic,
Outdoors on lawns, in trees,
        behind the bushes, in the garden,
        flowers, swings, trees, forts.

We grew here. We became ourselves.
Whether arriving from school or from a long trip,
We knew:
We were HOME.

Bobbi's Poem

The front porch.

The Back Yard.

Christmas. Family with train set.

Holy Rosary Church

Holy Rosary School

Denny Sheedy's Birthday with Russell and Nicky Criss and Us.

Our Dad.

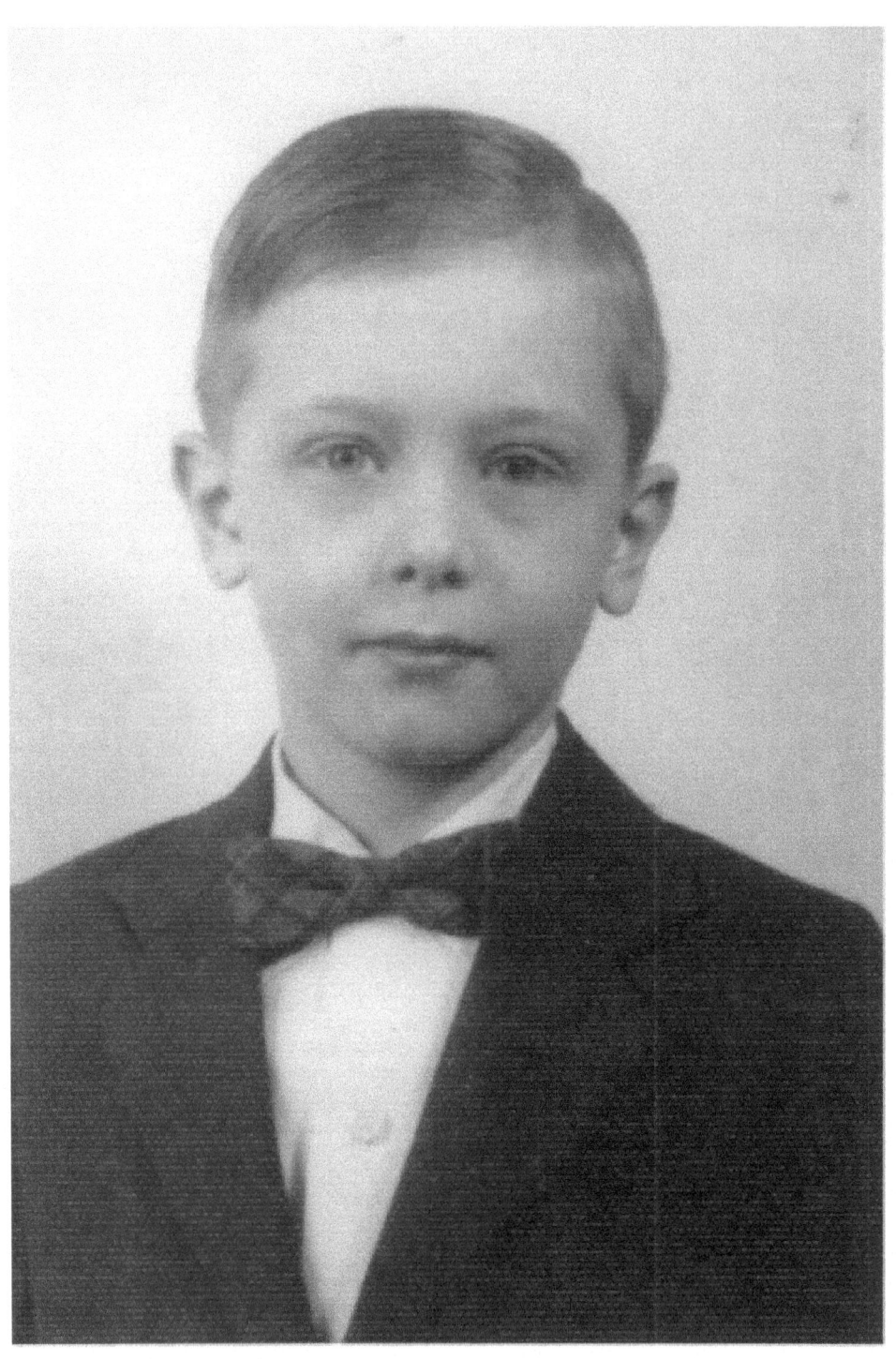

Holy Communion photo of Buddy.

Bobbi, Buddy, Maureen and Jimmy at Conneaut Lake.

Buddy and Bobbi on vacation.

Maureen at the front door.

Mom in the kitchen.

Mom getting into The Bomb.

Dad in The Bomb.

100% Jimmy

Informal Buddy.

www.ingramcontent.com/pod-product-compliance
Lightning Source LLC
Chambersburg PA
CBHW051206120626
46547CB00013B/1225